# Prayer

# Prayer

## The Breath of New Life

# POPE FRANCIS

WITH A PREFACE BY
PATRIARCH KIRILL OF MOSCOW AND ALL RUSSIA

Our Sunday Visitor
Huntington, Indiana

24 23 22 21 20 20      1 2 3 4 5 6 7 8 9

Published in English by Our Sunday Visitor Publishing Division, Our Sunday Visitor, Inc., 200 Noll Plaza, Huntington, IN 46750; 1-800-348-2440; www.osv.com.

ISBN: 978-1-68192-678-0 (Inventory No. T2549)
eISBN: 978-1-68192-679-7
LCCN: 2020939795

Cover design: Tyler Ottinger
Cover art: AdobeStock
Interior design: Amanda Falk

PRINTED IN THE UNITED STATES OF AMERICA

# TABLE OF CONTENTS

• • •

• • •

# PREFACE

*+ Kirill*
*Patriarch of Moscow and All Russia*

Dear brothers and sisters!

*Prayer: The Breath of New Life!* This book presents a fine selection of reflections, quotes, and catechetical speeches by Pope Francis on Christian prayer.

Since the day of his election to the papacy on March 13, 2013, both in official and unofficial settings, as well as in gatherings with the Christian faithful, Francis has made the same appeal: "Pray for me!" This alone testifies to the importance he places on prayer. Obviously, a book like this bears the imprint of the pontiff's personal prayer habits. But this makes it anything but abstract. It is based on real, lived experience.

This is how Francis defines the essence of prayer: "Above all, it is a dialogue and a personal relationship with God. Man was created in a personal relationship with God, and he therefore reaches his full potential only in an encounter with his Creator." Indeed, if we pray with a pure heart, we will encounter God; we will feel the true presence of Our Lord next to us; we converse with him, and he responds to us by speaking in a wholly unique way.

Prayer unites the human person with others. Prayer connects a Christian to his brothers and sisters in the Faith who are lifted up to heaven in prayer. This is felt in a special way in the Liturgy of the Hours, the official prayer of the universal Church, through which the Savior, as promised, is present among those gathered in his name (cf. Mt 18:20). This divine presence can be felt by everyone through the particular experience of grace that envelops us whenever we enter the Lord's house.

Pope Francis has noted several times that the first person singular "I" is never used in the Our Father, the prayer the Lord himself taught us. This is because each of us presents the prayer to our heavenly Father on behalf of all humanity. I think this is an extremely important observation since we live in a time when interpersonal communication is in a crisis. Globalization has made the world more open and united, but this does not mean that individual human beings have felt closer to one another. We live in a time plagued with individualism, in which people seek to satisfy their own desires and needs and are increasingly indifferent to the problems of others. The inability to sympathize with others, to care about their needs, leads to a plethora of disorders in social relations and the disintegration of the family, even Christian families. To a large degree, this is due to a weakening of the faith and a lack of prayer, or at least their distortion into a form of psychotherapy and a method for self-soothing. What prayer really brings us is the divine grace that helps us overcome egoism and grow in love for our neighbors.

A great saint of the Russian Orthodox Church, Theophan the Recluse (1815–94), reflecting on personal prayer in the home, wrote: "The Lord asks very little of us, but that little we do must come from the heart. In this case, a simple, 'Lord, have mercy,' can be sufficient" (*Letters,* nos. 293, 417). In this ancient little prayer, we invoke the Lord's mercy upon ourselves and everyone whom we love and for whom we intercede by praying in his presence.

In his reflections on prayer, Pope Francis points out another aspect of authenticity: "Prayer ... is work: a work that demands our will, dedication, and determination." Indeed, our human limitations and sinfulness do not always dispose us to prayer. But if we overcome these thanks to prayer, it is precisely because it naturally required some effort.

Based on their experience of asceticism, the ancient Fathers of the Church teach us how to practice the habit of prayer in a way that it becomes pleasing to God. "May everyone pray attentively and conscientiously, not allowing their minds to wander arbitrarily and not viewing prayer as a necessary debt, but rather filling it with love and accepting it as a desire of the soul," Saint Gregory of Nyssa taught in the fourth century.[1]

Prayer can indeed become tiresome, so we must muster perseverance and discipline. Pope Francis teaches us that "prayer changes reality ... it either changes things or it changes our hearts." Prayer, practiced faithfully and regularly, surely cannot be anything but efficacious as it transforms both us and the reality around us, as the Lord taught: "Ask and you shall receive, seek and you shall find, knock and the door will be opened to you" (Mt 7:8).

Torn by conflict and rivalry, our world is in such need of Christian prayer. As followers of Christ, it is essential for us to pray "for the peace of the whole world, for the well-being of God's Holy Churches, and for the unity of all peoples" (cf. the Great Intercession of the Byzantine Rite). When I met with His Holiness Pope Francis in Havana in 2016, we expressed our common hope that the historic accord would "inspire Christians throughout the world to pray to the Lord with renewed fervor for the unity of all his disciples" (*Joint Declaration*, 6). In the hope that our appeal and our prayers may be heard, I welcome the publication of this book in which we read how Francis understands prayer as the heart of Christian life.

# A FEW SENTENCES ON PRAYER

When faced with those who lack goodwill, with those who seek nothing but scandal, who seek only division, who seek only destruction, even within families: our silence alone is a response. And prayer.[1]

Yes, there are miracles. But prayer will always have its place! Courageous prayer, struggling prayer, persistent prayer, not a simply courteous prayer.[2]

Let us pray for a heart that embraces immigrants. God will judge us on the basis of how we have treated those most in need.[3]

And I pray. I pray in my own way. I really like the breviary and I never put it aside. I celebrate Mass every day. The

Rosary ... when I pray, I always pick up the Bible. And peace wells up in my heart. I don't know if this is a secret ... my peace is a gift of the Lord. May he never take it away![4]

Without the Holy Spirit — we know well — there is no possibility of a good life, nor of changing our lives. We pray and dedicate ourselves to keep his strength within us so that "the world of our time ... may receive the Good News ... from the ministers of the Gospel whose lives glow with fervor" (Paul VI, *Evangelii Nuntiandi,* 80).[5]

Think about the priestly prayer of Jesus when he prays to the Father: "I do not ask that you take them out of the world but that you keep them from the evil one" (Jn 17:15). Worldliness works against witness, while the spirit of prayer is witness that can be seen: a man or woman dedicated to prayer can be recognized, as well as the person who utters the formulas but does not pray with his heart. These are testimonies that people can indeed see.[6]

A family who prays together stays together.[7]

Be on the attack in your prayer. Do not grow slack. ... Prayer is work: a work that requires will, consistency, and determination, shedding all bashfulness. Why? Because I am knocking at the door of my friend. God is a friend, and I can act this way with a friend. Prayer needs to be constant and persistent.[8]

Our lives change when we take on the habit of prayer.[9]

# UNITED WITH JESUS

## JESUS PRAYS FOR US[1]

Jesus said to Peter: "Simon, Simon, behold Satan has demanded to sift all of you like wheat, but I have prayed that your own faith may not fail; and once you have turned back, you must strengthen your brothers" (Lk 22:31–32).

Taking this passage from Luke's Gospel as our guide, we notice what it is that Satan demands "to sift" in Peter, how Jesus prays for Peter's weakness, and how sin can be transformed into grace and indeed become a grace for the whole community.

Let's focus on the verb "to sift" (*siniazo* in Greek: "to sift out sand"), which evokes the movement of the Spirit, thanks to whom, in the end, we discern what is of a good spirit and what is of a bad one. In this case, the person who sifts — the one who appropriates the power to sift — is the evil spirit. The Lord does not prevent this, but, taking advantage of the "test," he prays to the Father that Simon Peter's heart may be strengthened. Jesus prays that Peter's faith may not fail; that is, that *he may not be put to the test.* In his passion, the Lord did everything possible to protect those who belong to him. But he cannot prevent the possibility of someone being tempted by the Devil, who always has our greatest weakness in his sights. In this type of trial — a trial that Jesus does not cause directly but also does not impede — Paul tells us that the Lord sees to it that we are not tempted beyond our strength (cf. 1 Cor 10:13).

The fact that the Lord says explicitly that he is praying for Simon is extremely important, because the most insidious temptation that Satan can lure us with is that — in the midst of a particular trial — he makes us feel that Jesus has abandoned us, that he has left us alone and not helped us as he should. The Lord himself experienced and overcame this temptation, first in the garden and then on the cross, entrusting himself to the Father's hands when he felt abandoned. It is at this point that we need our faith to be strengthened and affirmed in a special way and with special care. We find the very strength we need in the fact that the Lord alludes to what will happen to Simon Peter and assures him that he has already prayed for him so that his faith might not fail.

As we see in this exchange with Peter, the "eclipse" of faith that can occur when faced with the scandal of the Passion is something the Lord prays about in a special way. He asks that we pray always and with persistence. He unites us to his prayer and teaches us to beg that "we may not fall into temptation," and that we may "be freed from evil," since we know our flesh is weak. The Lord also reveals that there are demons that cannot be overcome except by prayer and penance, and he shows us that he prays for our temptations in a special way. The episode about Peter is an example of that. Just as he had reserved to himself the humble gesture of washing his disciples' feet and personally consoled his disciples after his resurrection, so this prayer, with which he strengthens the faith of Simon Peter and strengthens the faith of others, is something the Lord embraces as his personal mission. We must not forget: If we want our faith to be stronger, we must turn to this prayer which the Lord offered once and continues to offer ("he stands at the Father's right hand to intercede for us," Rom 8:34).

If the lesson the Lord gave to Simon Peter to allow his feet to be washed affirmed the Lord's attitude of service and fixed it firmly within the Church's memory as a fundamental act, we must also embrace this lesson as a symbol of the tried and true faith the Lord prays for in us. As priests who take part in the Petrine ministry, we participate in the same mission: We must not only wash the feet of our brothers and sisters on Holy Thursday, we must also strengthen them in the Faith, witnessing how the Lord prayed for our faith.

If the Lord strengthens and encourages us in the trials of the flesh — often performing incredible miracles of healing — in the trials that come directly from the Devil, the Lord adopts a more complex strategy. We notice that the Lord expels some demons directly without engaging them. At other times he neutralizes them, demanding they keep silent. Sometimes he makes them speak or asks them their name, as he did with the spirit who identified itself as "Legion." At other times he responds to them with ample quotes from Scripture, engaging them for some time, as he did when he fought temptation in the desert. In the case of this "demon," who tempts his friend right before Jesus enters his passion, it is defeated by prayer: praying not that the spirit leave him in peace, but that his harassing might become a source of strength and benefit for others.

In this scriptural passage, we have some wonderful lessons to learn about the growth of faith. The first regards the scandal of the Innocent One's suffering and the suffering of the innocents. This touches us more deeply than we realize, for it touches upon those who provoke him and those who pretend not to see. It behooves us to listen to the words of the Lord just at that moment when he begins to take upon himself the scandal of the Passion, that he prays that the one provoked may not fail, and that he indeed will be able to strengthen others in the faith. The eclipse of faith provoked by the passion is not something that anyone can solve or overcome individually.

## THE NEED FOR FAITH

Indeed,[2] let us remember what the Lord Jesus told us: "If you abide in me, and my words abide in you, ask whatever you will, and it shall be done for you" (Jn 15:7). "But we do not believe this, because we have little faith." But — as Jesus says — if we had faith like the mustard seed, we would have received all. "Ask whatever you will, and it shall be done for you." In the Mass, the moment of universal prayer after the Creed is the time to ask the Lord for the most important things, the things we need most, the things we most want. "It shall be done for you"; in one way or another, "it shall be done for you." "All things are possible to him who believes," the Lord said. How did the man respond to whom the Lord had addressed the words: "All things are possible to him who believes"? He responded: "I believe, Lord. Help my little faith." We too can say: "Lord, I believe. But help my lack of faith." We must pray with this spirit of faith: "I believe, Lord; help my lack of faith." Worldly demands, however, do not ascend toward heaven, just as self-referential requests remain unheard (cf. Jas 4:2–3). The intentions for which the faithful people are invited to pray must give voice to the concrete needs of the ecclesial community and the world, avoiding recourse to conventional and shortsighted formulas. The "universal" prayer that concludes the Liturgy of the Word exhorts us to turn our gaze to God who takes care of his children.

## THE COURAGE OF PRAYER

How do we pray?[3] Do we pray out of habit, devoutly, peacefully, or do we place ourselves courageously before the Lord and ask him for his grace? Do we ask him for something really concrete? ... A prayer that is not courageous ... is not a true prayer. ... The Lord tells us as much, because he assures us that whoever asks receives, whoever searches finds, and whoever knocks will have the door opened. ... Do we allow ourselves to get caught up in prayer? Do we know how to knock on the door of the Lord's heart? ... Jesus tells us: "What father among you would hand his son a snake when he asks for a fish? Or hand him a scorpion when he asks for an egg? If you then, who are wicked, know how to give good gifts to your children, how much more will the Father in heaven ... " (Lk 11:11–13). We would expect him to close the phrase by saying, " ... will give good things to you." But he doesn't! Rather, he says, " ... will the Father in heaven give the holy Spirit to those who ask Him" (v. 13). And this is indeed something great. ... When we pray courageously, the Lord does not only give us grace; he gives us himself in grace. ... The Lord ... never gives or sends a grace through the mail: He himself brings it, because he himself is grace!

Today ... in the opening prayer, we ask the Lord to give us what prayer itself does not dare to ask. And what is this thing we don't dare ask for? God himself! We ask for some particular grace, but we don't dare say: Come, bring it yourself! We know that grace is always from him: it is he who comes and gives it to us. So may we never be so callous as to take a grace but not recognize the one who brings it, the one who gives it: the Lord himself.

## GOD'S "MORE"

It is characteristic of God's mercy not only to pardon but also to be generous and to give more and more.[4] ... We often ask for this or that specific thing in prayer, but he always ends up giving us more! Always much, much more. ... Properly speaking, this is what prayer is: seeking the "how" and knocking on the door of God's heart, who is a friend always with us, the Father himself. ... "If you then, who are wicked, know how to give good gifts to your children, how much more will the Father in heaven give the Holy Spirit to those who ask him" (Lk 11:13). Yes! He will give the Holy Spirit to those who ask him! ... This is the gift, this is God's "more."

... He will never give you a gift, something that you ask him for, without wrapping it well, and without something that will make it all the more beautiful. ... What the Lord gives us — the "more" that the Father always give us — is the Spirit: the true gift of the Father and that which prayer does not dare hope for. ... He who is Father gives me that and gives me more: the gift, the Holy Spirit. ... Our prayer must therefore be trinitarian. ... The Father exists, as does the Son and the Holy Spirit. They are *persons.* They are not noble ideas floating in the air. ... Jesus is our companion on the journey who gives us what we ask for. The Father cares for us and loves us. The Holy Spirit, who is the gift, is the "more" that the Father gives us, that which our conscience does not dare hope for.

## THE HOLY SPIRIT ALLOWS US TO MEET THE FATHER

"Father."[5] This is the key to prayer. We cannot pray unless we use the word and sense its meaning. Jesus promises us the Holy Spirit. It is the Spirit who teaches us in the depths of our hearts to say, "Father," and to say, "Our" ... by making peace with our enemies.

## JESUS INVITES US TO PRAY[6]

The Gospel presents Jesus in dialogue with his Father. It brings us to the heart of the prayerful intimacy between the Father and the Son. As his hour drew near, Jesus prayed for his disciples, for those with him, and for those who were yet to come (cf. Jn 17:20). We do well to remember that, in that crucial moment, Jesus made the lives of his disciples, our lives, a part of his prayer. He asked his Father to keep them united and joyful. Jesus knew full well the hearts of his disciples, and he knows full well our own. And so he prays to the Father to save them from a spirit of isolation, of finding refuge in their own certainties and comfort zones, of indifference to others and division into "cliques" which disfigure the richly diverse face of the Church. These are situations which lead to a kind of isolation and ennui, a sadness that slowly gives rise to resentment, to constant complaint, to boredom; this "is not God's will for us, nor is it the life in the Spirit" (*Evangelii Gaudium*, 2) to which he invited them, to which he has invited us. That is why Jesus prays that sadness and isolation will not prevail in our hearts. We want to do the same, we want to join in Jesus' prayer, in his words, so that we can say together: "Father, keep them in your name ... that they may be one, even as we are one" (Jn 17:11), "that your joy may be complete" (Jn 15:11).

Jesus prays, and he invites us to pray, because he knows that some things can only be received as gifts; some things can only be experienced as gifts. Unity is a grace which can be bestowed upon us only by the Holy Spirit; we have to ask for this grace and do our best to be transformed by that gift. ...

The Lord prays also that we may be filled with his own "complete joy" (cf. Jn 17:13). The joy of Christians, and especially of consecrated men and women, is a very clear sign of Christ's presence in their lives. When we see sad faces, it is a warning that something is wrong. Significantly, this is the request which Jesus makes of the Father just before he goes out to the Garden to renew his own "fiat." I am certain that all of you have had to bear many sacrifices, and, for some of you, for several decades now, these sacrifices have proved difficult. Jesus prays, at the moment of his own sacrifice, that we will never lose the joy of knowing that he overcomes the world. This certainty is what inspires us, morning after morning, to renew our faith. "With a tenderness which never disappoints, but is always capable of restoring our joy" — by his prayer, and in the faces of our people — Christ "makes it possible for us to lift up our heads and to start anew" (*Evangelii Gaudium*, 3). ...

Dear brothers and sisters, Jesus prays that all of us may be one, and that his joy may abide within us. May we do likewise, as we unite ourselves to one another in prayer.

## LEAVING SPACE FOR GOD[7]

The Gospel this Sunday (Lk 11:1–13) opens with the scene of Jesus, who is praying alone, apart from the others; when he finishes, the disciples ask him, "Lord, teach us to pray" (v. 1). He says in reply, "When you pray, say: 'Father ... '" (v. 2). This word is the "secret" of Jesus' prayer, it is the key that he himself gives to us so that we too might enter into that relationship of confidential dialogue with the Father who accompanied and sustained his whole life.

With the name "Father" Jesus combines two requests: "hallowed be thy name, thy kingdom come" (v. 2). Jesus' prayer, and the Christian prayer therefore, first and foremost, makes room for God, allowing him to show his holiness in us and to advance his kingdom, beginning with the possibility of exercising his Lordship of love in our lives.

Three other supplications complete this prayer that Jesus taught — that is, the "Our Father." There are three questions that express our basic needs: *bread, forgiveness*, and *help in temptation* (cf. vv. 3–4). One cannot live without bread, one cannot live without forgiveness, and one cannot live without God's help in times of temptation. The *bread* that Jesus teaches us to ask for is what is necessary, not superfluous. It is the bread of pilgrims, the righteous, a bread that is neither accumulated nor wasted, and that does not weigh us down as we walk. *Forgiveness* is, above all, what we ourselves receive from God: only the awareness that we are sinners forgiven by God's infinite mercy can enable us to carry out concrete gestures of fraternal reconciliation. If a person does not feel that he/she is a sinner who has been forgiven, that person will never be able to make a gesture of forgiveness or reconciliation. It begins in the heart where you feel that you are a forgiven sinner. The last supplication, *"lead us not into temptation,"* expresses the awareness of our condition, which is always exposed to the snares of evil and corruption. We all know what temptation is!

Jesus' teaching on prayer continues with two parables, which he modeled on the behavior of a friend toward another friend, and that of a father toward his son (cf. vv. 5–12). Both are intended to teach us to have *full confidence in God,* who is Father. He knows our needs better than we do ourselves, but he wants us to present them to him *boldly and persistently,* because this is our way of participating in his work of salvation. *Prayer is the first and principle "working instrument" we have in our hands!* In being persistent with God, we don't need to convince him, but to strengthen our faith and our patience, meaning our ability to strive together with God for the things that are truly important and necessary. In prayer there are two of us: God and I, striving together for the important things.

Among these, there is one, the great important thing that Jesus speaks of in today's Gospel, which we almost never ask for, and that is *the Holy Spirit*. "Give me the Holy Spirit ... !" And Jesus says, "If you then, who are evil, know how to give good gifts to your children, how much more will the heavenly Father give the Holy Spirit to those who ask him for it!" (v. 13). The Holy Spirit! We must ask that the Holy Spirit comes within us. But what is the use of the Holy Spirit? We need him to live well, to live with wisdom and love, doing God's will. What a beautiful prayer it would be if, this week, each of us were to ask the Father: "Father, give me the Holy Spirit!" Our Lady demonstrates this with her life, which was entirely enlivened by the Spirit of God. May she, united to Jesus, help us to pray to the Father so that we might not live in a worldly manner, but according to the Gospel, guided by the Holy Spirit.

## DWELLING IN THE LORD'S PRESENCE[8]

I pray the Divine Office every morning. I like to pray the Psalms. After that, I celebrate Mass. I also pray the Rosary. What I prefer most is evening adoration, even when I feel distracted or my thoughts wander or fall asleep while praying. In the evening, between 7:00 p.m. and 8:00 p.m., I am there before the Most Holy Sacrament for an hour of adoration. But I also pray mentally when I'm waiting for the dentist or when busy during the day. For me, prayer consists in a kind of "memory": memories of my personal history or of what the Lord has done for his Church or for some particular parish. This, I think, is what Saint Ignatius means when he talks about exercising the "memory" in the first week of the *Spiritual Exercises.* He puts it in terms of a merciful encounter with the Crucified Christ. I then ask myself: "What have I done for Christ? What am I doing for Christ? When must I do for Christ?" Ignatius also talks about this kind of memory in the *Contemplatio ad amorem* in which he invites us to recall the benefits we have received from him. Above all, I know the Lord remembers me. I can forget him, but I know he loves me and can never forget me. "Memory" is the radical core of Jesuit spirituality: it consists in remembering grace. It is the memory spoken of in the Book of Deuteronomy, the memory of God's works that are the basis for the covenant between God and his people. It is this "memory" that makes me a son of God and makes me a father.

## WE LEARN HOW TO PRAY WITH OUR BROTHERS AND SISTERS IN THE LITURGY[9]

To illustrate the beauty of the Eucharistic celebration, I would like to begin with a very simple aspect: Mass is prayer; it is prayer *par excellence*, the loftiest, the most sublime, and at the same time the most "concrete." In fact, it is the loving encounter with God through his word and the Body and Blood of Jesus. It is an encounter with the Lord.

But first we must answer a question. What truly is prayer? It is first of all a dialogue, a personal relationship with God. Man was created as a being in a personal relationship with God who finds his complete fulfillment only in the encounter with his Creator. The path of life leads toward the definitive encounter with the Lord.

The Book of Genesis states that man was created in the

image and likeness of God, who is the Father and Son and Holy Spirit, a perfect relationship of love which is unity. From this we can understand that we were all created in order to enter a perfect relationship of love, in the continuous giving and receiving of ourselves so as to be able to find the fulfillment of our being.

When Moses, before the burning bush, receives God's call, he asks him his name. And how does God respond? "I am who I am" (Ex 3:14). This expression, in its original sense, expresses *presence and favor*, and immediately afterward God adds: "the Lord, the God of your fathers, the God of Abraham, of Isaac, and of Jacob" (v. 15). Thus, when Christ calls his disciples, he, too, calls them so that they may be *with him*. This indeed is the greatest grace: being able to feel that the Mass, the Eucharist, is the privileged moment to be with Jesus and, through him, with God and with brothers and sisters.

Praying, as every true dialogue, is also knowing how to be in silence — in dialogues there are moments of silence — in silence together with Jesus. When we go to Mass, perhaps we arrive five minutes early and begin to chat with the person next to us. But this is not the moment for small talk; it is the moment of silence to prepare ourselves for the dialogue. It is the moment for recollection within the heart, to prepare ourselves for the encounter with Jesus. Silence is so important! Remember what I said last week: We are not going to a spectacle, we are going to the encounter with the Lord, and silence prepares us and accompanies us. Pausing in silence with Jesus. From this mysterious silence of God springs his word, which resonates in our heart. Jesus himself teaches us how it is truly possible to "be" with the Father, and he shows us this with his prayer. The Gospels show us a Jesus who withdraws to secluded places to pray; seeing his intimate relationship with God, the disciples feel the desire to be able to take part in it, and they ask him, "Lord, teach us to pray" (Lk 11:1). We heard it in the first Reading, at the beginning of the audience. Jesus responds that the first thing necessary for prayer is being able to say "Father." Let us take heed: If I am not able to say "Father" to God, I am not capable of prayer. We must learn to say "Father" — that is, to place ourselves in his presence with filial trust. But to be able to learn, we must humbly recognize that we need to be taught, and to say with simplicity, "Lord, teach me to pray."

This is the first point: to be humble, to recognize ourselves as children, to rest in the Father, to trust in him. To enter the kingdom of heaven it is necessary to become little, like children. In the sense that children know how to trust; they know that someone will take care of them, of what they will eat, of what they will wear, and so on (cf. Mt 6:25-32). This is the first perspective: *trust and confidence*, as a child toward his parents; to know that God remembers you, takes care of you, of you, of me, of everyone.

The second condition, too, is being precisely like children; it is to let ourselves be surprised. A child always asks thousands of questions because he wants to discover the world; and he even marvels at little things because everything is new to him. To enter the kingdom of heaven we must let ourselves be astonished. In our relationship with the Lord, in prayer — I ask — do we let ourselves be astonished, or do we think that prayer is speaking with God as parrots do? No, it is trusting and opening the heart so as to let ourselves be astonished. Do we allow ourselves to be surprised by God, who is always the God of surprises? Because the encounter with the Lord is always a living encounter; it is not a museum encounter. It is a living encounter, and we go to Mass, not to a museum. We go to a living encounter with the Lord.

The Gospel speaks of a certain Nicodemus (cf. Jn 3:1–21), an elderly man, an authority in Israel, who goes to Jesus to get to know him; and the Lord speaks to him of the need to "be born anew" (cf. v. 3). But what does it mean? Can one be "reborn"? Is it possible to return to having the zest, the joy, the wonder of life, even in the face of so much tragedy? This is a fundamental question of our faith, and this is the longing of every true believer: the longing to be reborn, the joy of beginning anew. Do we have this longing? Does each of us have the wish to be born ever anew in order to meet the Lord? Do you have this wish? Indeed, one can easily lose it because, due to so many activities, so many projects to implement, in the end we are short of time and we lose sight of what is fundamental: the inner life of the heart, our spiritual life, our life which is the encounter with the Lord in prayer.

In truth, the Lord surprises us by showing us that he loves us even in our weaknesses. "Jesus Christ ... is the expiation for our sins, and not for ours only but also for the sins of the whole world" (1 Jn 2:2). This gift, the source of true consolation — but the Lord always forgives us — this consoles; it is a true consolation; it is a gift that we are given through the Eucharist, that wedding feast at which the Bridegroom encounters our frailty. Can I say that when I receive Communion during Mass, the Lord encounters my frailty? Yes!

We can say so because this is true! The Lord encounters our frailty so as to lead us back to our first call: that of being in the image and likeness of God. This is the environment of the Eucharist. This is prayer.

## BECOMING MORE LIKE JESUS[10]

Liturgical prayer, in its unhurried structure, is meant to be an expression of the whole Church, the Spouse of Christ, as she strives to be ever more conformed to her Lord. Each one of us, in prayer, wants to become more like Jesus.

Prayer expresses what we experience and what we ought to experience in our daily lives. At least that is true of prayer that is not self-centered or merely for show. Prayer makes us put into practice, or examine our consciences about, what we have prayed for in the Psalms. We are the hands of the God who "lifts up the poor from the dust" (Ps 112:7). We work to turn what is dry and barren into the joy of fertile ground. We cry out that "precious in the eyes of the Lord is the life of his faithful ones." We are those who fight, speak up and defend the dignity of every human life, from conception to old age, when our years are many and our strength fails. Prayer is the reflection of our love for God, for others, and for all creation. The commandment of love is the greatest way for the missionary disciple to be conformed to Jesus. Union with Jesus deepens our Christian vocation, which is concerned with what Jesus "does" — which is something much greater than mere "activities" — with becoming more like him in all that we do. The beauty of the ecclesial community is born of this union of each of her members to the person of Jesus, creating an "ensemble of vocations" in the richness of harmonic diversity.

## ADORATION[11]

To adore. We, in this world of efficiency, have lost the meaning of adoration, including in prayer. It is true, we pray, we praise the Lord, we ask, we thank. ... However, adoration is being before the One God, the One who is above price, who does not barter, who does not exchange. ... And everything that is outside of him is a "cardboard imitation," an idol. ... To adore. In this we must make an effort to grow in this way of prayer: adoration. Adore, adore God. This is lacking in the Church at this moment, because it is not taught. This sense of adoration that we see in the Bible in the First Commandment — "Adore the one God. You will have no other God. He is the Only One you must adore ... " This "wasting time" without asking, without praising, also without giving thanks, only adoring, with the soul prostrated. I don't know why I feel like saying this to you, but I feel I must say it to you; it comes from within me.

## ENTRUSTING EVERYTHING TO GOD[12]

Prayer then is not a nice practice for finding a little peace of heart; nor is it a means of devotion for obtaining useful things from God. Were it so, then it would be an act of subtle selfishness: I pray in order to be well, just as if taking an aspirin. But this is just making a deal. No, it's not like this. Prayer is something else, it is something else. Prayer is instead *a spiritual work of mercy*, which means bringing everything to the heart of God. "You take it, you who are Father." It should be like this, speaking to him in a simple way. Prayer is saying: "You, take it, you who are Father. Look at us, you who are Father." This is the relationship with the Father. Prayer is like this. It is a gift of faith and love, an intercession needed just as bread is. In a word, it means *to entrust*: entrust the Church, entrust people, entrust situations to the Father — "I entrust this to you" — so that you will take care of it. That is why prayer, as Padre Pio liked to say, is "the greatest weapon we have, a key that opens the heart of God." A key that opens God's heart: it is a simple key. The heart of God is not "heavily guarded" with many security measures. You can open it with a common key, with prayer. For his is a heart of love, a father's heart. And it is the Church's greatest strength, one which we must never let go of, for the Church bears fruit only if she does as did Our Lady and the apostles, who "with one accord devoted themselves to prayer" (Acts 1:14) as they awaited the Holy Spirit. Dedicated and united in prayer. Otherwise we risk relying elsewhere for support: on means, on money, on power; then evangelization vanishes and joy is extinguished and the heart grows dull. Do you want to have a dull heart? [*the people respond*: No!] Do you want to have a joyful heart? [Yes!] Pray! This is the recipe.

## WITH COURAGE[13]
In today's liturgy, Mark presents us with a healing: Jesus heals. ... This reminds us ... of what Scripture teaches about the role of prayer in asking a favor from the Lord by raising the prayer of this people as an example. ... When we ask something of the Lord, we must ask in faith. ... There was another man ... who asked Jesus to heal his son possessed by a demon. The man says to Jesus, "If you want to, you can do

something." Struck by these words, Jesus responds, "If you all had faith the size of a mustard seed." Jesus replies to the doubting man that *everything is possible to the one who believes.* But the poor man anxiously replies, "I believe, Lord, but help my weak faith!" ... When we approach the Lord to ask something, we must do it with deep faith: I have faith that you can heal me, I believe that you can do this. ... Prayer in faith. ... How do I pray? When I need something, how do I ask him? Do I ask it in faith, or do I ask it rather like a parrot? Do I simply repeat again and again, "Lord, I need this!" ... I am really invested in what I am asking for? Or is it more, "Well, if he gives it, great, and if not, too bad." No, this is simply not the way to go about it. ...

If I ask for something, the prayer must begin with faith. If I don't have much faith, we can respond like the child's father in the Gospel: "I believe, Lord, but help my little faith!" ... We often ... encounter difficulties. ... In the Gospel today, they arrive with a paralyzed man on a mat and encounter a crowd both inside and outside the house, and they can hardly get near ... so they go behind the house and get on the roof. They make a hole in it and lower the mat down to Jesus. ... There was a problem and they knew how to look beyond the problem and seek a way to get the man close to Jesus with the faith that he had the power to heal. ... They had the courage to seek another way.

There are many people like this in the Gospel. ... We can think of the old woman who suffered a hemorrhage for eighteen years. Jesus was far off and there was a large crowd, but she says, "If I could only touch the fringe of his mantle, I will be saved." ... With a strong faith, she inserts herself into the crowd. She gets closer, closer, closer, and she touches him. ... Jesus notices, and she is healed. ... The courage to fight and reach the Lord, the courage to have faith from the beginning: "If you want to, you can heal me. I believe you can if you want to." ... The courage to get close to the Lord, whenever we are overwhelmed with problems. ... That courage: often we need patience and know how to wait until the right time, but we never give up. We always move forward. ... Think of Saint Monica and how she prayed, crying for the conversion of her son Augustine. And through prayer she obtained it. ... We need to play hardball when we pray, and if there are difficulties, we overcome them, just as these exemplary people of faith.

Christian prayer ... is born from our faith in Jesus, and in faith prayer always overcomes difficulties. ... There is a passage from Scripture that can help us with this today. The apostle Paul tells us that our father in faith, Abraham, who received the promise of progeny at the age of a hundred years, "believed," and that through his faith he was justified. ... Faith is doing everything to obtain the grace that we ask. ... The Lord tells us, "Ask, and it will be given to you." Let us put our trust in his word and deepen our faith. But let us always put this faith into action. ... This is the precisely the kind of courage that characterizes Christian prayer: If prayer lacks courage, it is not Christian.

## WITH PERSISTENCE[14]

In today's Gospel Jesus tells a parable on the need to pray always, never wearying. The main character is a widow whose insistent pleading with a dishonest judge succeeds in obtaining justice from him. Jesus concludes that if the widow succeeded in convincing that judge, do you think that God will not listen to us if we pray to him with insistence? Jesus' words are very strong: "And will not God vindicate his elect, who cry to him day and night?" (Lk 18:7).

Crying day and night to God! This image of prayer is striking, but let us ask ourselves: Why does God want this? Doesn't he already know what we need? What does it mean to "insist" with God?

This is a good question that makes us examine an important aspect of the faith: God invites us to pray insistently not because he is unaware of our needs, or because he is not listening to us. On the contrary, he is always listening, and he knows everything about us lovingly. On our daily journey, especially in times of difficulty, in the battle against the evil that is outside and within us, the Lord is not far away, he is by our side. We battle with him beside us, and our weapon is prayer which makes us feel his presence beside us, his mercy, and also his help. But the battle against evil is a long and hard one; it requires patience and endurance, like Moses who had to keep his arms outstretched for the people to prevail (cf. Ex 17:8-13). This is how it is: There is a battle to be waged each day, but God is our ally; faith in him is our strength and prayer is the expression of this faith. Therefore, Jesus assures us of the victory, but at the end he asks: "When the Son of man comes, will he find faith on earth?" (Lk 18:8). If faith is snuffed out, prayer is snuffed out and we walk in the dark. We become lost on the path of life.

Therefore, let us learn from the widow of the Gospel to pray always without growing weary. This widow was very good! She knew how to battle for her children! I think of the many women who fight for their families, who pray and never grow weary. Today let us all remember these women who by their attitude provide us with a true witness of faith and courage, and a model of prayer. Our thoughts go out to them!

Pray always, but not in order to convince the Lord by dint of words! He knows our needs better than we do! Indeed, persevering prayer is the expression of faith in a God who calls us to fight with him every day and at every moment in order to conquer evil with good.

# WHEREVER YOU ARE, PRAY TO THE FATHER

From the catechesis on the Lord's Prayer*

## TEACHER, TEACH US HOW TO PRAY

The[1] Gospels have consigned to us very lively portrayals of Jesus as a man of prayer. Jesus prayed. Despite the urgency of his mission and the pressure from the many people making demands on him, Jesus feels the need to withdraw

---

* The following passages are taken from the catechesis on the Lord's Prayer, the Our Father, that Pope Francis gave during Wednesday General Audiences from December 2018 to May 2019. The catecheses are not given in full. Rather, selections are given that emphasize the theme of prayer in a special way. The texts in their entirety are available in Italian in a volume entitled *Scoprirsi figli di Dio. Catechesi sul Padre Nostro,* with a Preface by Walter Kasper (Vatican City State: Libreria Editrice Vaticana, 2019).

in solitude and pray. Mark's Gospel recounts this detail to us from the very first passage about Jesus' public ministry (cf. 1:35). Jesus' inaugural day in Capernaum has ended in a triumphant way. Once the sun has set, multitudes of sick people have reached the door where Jesus is staying: The Messiah preaches and heals. The ancient prophecies and expectations of so many suffering people are fulfilled: Jesus is the God-with-us, the God who frees us. But that crowd is still small when compared to the many other crowds that will gather around the prophet of Nazareth; at certain times the gatherings are oceanic, and Jesus is at the center of it all, the expectation of the peoples, the fulfillment of the hope of Israel.

Yet he slips away; he does not end up being a hostage to the expectations of those, who by then, had declared him a *leader*, which is a danger for leaders: to be too attached to people, not to keep their distance. Jesus realizes this and does not end up being a hostage to the people. From the very first night at Capernaum, he shows he is an original Messiah. At the end of the night, when dawn is already breaking, the disciples are still seeking him, but are unable to find him. Where is he? Until Peter at last tracks him down in an isolated place, completely absorbed in prayer. And Peter tells him: "Everyone is searching for you"! (Mk 1:37). The exclamation seems to be the appropriate phrase for an overwhelming success, proof of the successful outcome of a mission.

But Jesus says to his own that he must go elsewhere; that it is not the people who seek him, rather it is above all he who seeks others. He must therefore not put down roots but remain a constant pilgrim on the roads of Galilee (cf. vv. 38-

39), as well as a pilgrim toward the Father — that is, praying. On a journey of prayer, Jesus prays.

And it all happens during a night of prayer.

In some passages of Scripture it seems to be first and foremost Jesus' prayer, his intimacy with the Father, that governs everything. It is so, for example, especially on the night at Gethsemane. The final stretch of Jesus' journey (by far the most difficult of those he has undertaken thus far) seems to find its meaning in Jesus' continuous listening to the Father. Certainly not an easy prayer, indeed a truly "agonizing struggle" in the sense of the athletic spirit, yet a prayer, that is able to sustain the way of the cross.

Here is the essential point: *Jesus prayed* there.

Jesus prayed with intensity in public moments, sharing the liturgy of his people, but also seeking withdrawn places, away from the turbulence of the world, places that allowed him to dwell in the privacy of his soul: He is the prophet who knows the stones of the desert and goes up high into the mountains. Jesus' last words before dying on the cross are words from the psalms — that is, of prayer, the prayer of the Jews: He prayed with the prayers that his mother had taught him.

Jesus prayed like all men and women in the world pray. Yet his way of praying also contained a mystery, something that certainly did not escape the eyes of his disciples, since the Gospels contain that plea that was so simple and immediate: "Lord, teach us to pray" (Lk 11:1). They see Jesus praying, and they want to learn how to pray: "Lord, teach us to pray." And Jesus does not refuse, he is not possessive of his intimacy with the Father, but rather he came precisely to introduce us to this relationship with the Father. And thus he becomes the teacher of prayer to his disciples, as he undoubtedly wants to be so for all of us. We too should say: "Lord, teach me to pray. Teach me."

Even if we may have been praying for many years, we still have to learn! Man's prayer, this yearning which arises so naturally from his soul, is perhaps one of the deepest mysteries of the universe. And we do not even know whether the prayers that we address to God are effectively those that he wants to have addressed to him. The Bible also gives us testimonies of inappropriate prayers, which in the end are rejected by God: It is sufficient to recall the parable of the Pharisee and the tax collector. Only the latter, the publican, goes home from the Temple justified, because the Pharisee was proud, and he liked people to see him praying and he feigned prayer: the heart was cold. And Jesus says, this is not justified, "for every one who exalts himself will be humbled, but he who humbles himself will be exalted" (Lk 18:14). The first step to prayer is to be humble, to go to the Father and to say, "Look at me, I am a sinner, I am weak, I am bad": each one knows what to say. But one always begins with humility, and the Lord listens. The Lord listens to humble prayer.

Therefore, on beginning this series of catecheses on the prayer of Jesus, the most beautiful and just thing that we all must do is to repeat the disciples' appeal: "Teacher, teach us to pray!" It would be beautiful during this season of Advent to repeat, "Lord, teach me to pray." We can all go somewhat beyond this and pray better; but asking the Lord, "Lord, teach me to pray." Let us do this during this season of Advent and he will certainly not allow our invocation to go unheard.

## ASKING WITH TRUST

Let[2] us continue on the path of catecheses on the Lord's Prayer, which we began last week. Jesus places on the lips of his disciples a short, audacious prayer, made up of seven requests — a number that, in the Bible, is not random, but indicates fullness. I say audacious because, had Christ not suggested it, probably none of us — indeed, none of the most well-known theologians — would dare pray to God in this way.

In fact, Jesus invites his disciples to approach God and to confidently address several requests to him: first in regard to him and then in regard to us. There is no preamble to the Our Father. Jesus does not teach formulas for one to "ingratiate oneself" to the Lord, but instead invites us to pray to him by knocking down the barriers of awe and fear. He does not tell us we should address God by calling him "Almighty," "Most High," [by saying,] "You, who are so distant from us, I am a wretched man": No, he does not say this, but simply "Father," with total simplicity, as children address their father. And this word, "Father," expresses confidence and filial trust.

The Our Father prayer sinks its roots in the concrete reality of mankind. For example, it has us ask for bread, daily bread: a simple but essential request, which indicates that faith is not a matter of an "adornment," detached from life, which arises when all other needs have been satisfied. If anything, prayer begins with life itself. Prayer, Jesus teaches us, does not begin in human life after the stomach is full: rather, it settles in wherever a person is, anyone who is hungry, who weeps, who struggles, who suffers and who wonders why. Our first prayer, in a certain sense, was the wail that accompanied the first breath. In that newborn's cry the fate of our whole life was announced: our constant hunger, our constant thirst, our search for happiness.

In prayer, Jesus does not seek to extinguish the person; he does not seek to anesthetize him or her. He does not want us to tone down the demands and requests, learning to bear all things. Instead, he wants all suffering, all distress to soar heavenward and become dialogue.

Having faith, someone said, is a habit of crying out.

We all need to be like Bartimaeus in the Gospel (cf. Mk 10:46-52) — let us recall that passage of the Gospel: Bartimaeus, the son of Timaeus — that blind man who was begging at the gates of Jericho. He had so many good people around him telling him to keep quiet: "Be quiet! The Lord is passing by. Be quiet. Do not disturb. The Master has much to do; do not disturb him. You are annoying with your cries. Do not disturb." But he did not heed those suggestions: With blessed persistence, he insisted that his wretched condition might finally encounter Jesus. And he cried louder! And the polite people said: "No, he is the Master, please! You are making a bad impression!" And he cried out because he wanted to see; he wanted to be healed. "Jesus, have mercy on me!" (cf. v. 47). Jesus heals his sight and says, "Your faith has made you well" (v. 52), as if to explain that the decisive element of his healing was that prayer, that *invocation shouted out* with faith, stronger than the "common sense" of many people who wanted him to keep quiet. Prayer not only precedes salvation, but in some way already contains it, because it frees one from the despair of those who do not believe in a way out of many unbearable situations.

Of course, then, believers also feel the need to praise God. The Gospels offer us the jubilant exclamation that gushes forth from Jesus' heart, full of wonder, grateful to the Father (cf. Mt 11:25-27). The first Christians even felt the need to add a doxology to the text of the Lord's Prayer: "For thine is the power and the glory for ever" (*Didache*, 8:2).

But none of us is obliged to embrace the theory that someone advanced in the past — namely, that the prayer of supplication may be a weak form of faith, while the more authentic prayer would be pure praise, that which seeks God without the burden of any request. No, this is not true. The prayer of supplication is authentic; it is spontaneous; it is an act of faith in God who is Father, who is good, who is almighty. It is an act of faith in me, who am small, sinful, needy. And for this reason prayer, in order to ask for something, is quite noble. God is the Father who has immense compassion for us and wants his children to speak to him without fear, directly calling him "Father"; or amid difficulties saying, "Lord, what have you done to me?" For this reason we can tell him everything, even the things that are distorted and incomprehensible in our life. And he promised us that he would be with us for ever, until the last day we shall spend on this earth. Let us pray the Our Father, beginning this way, simply: "Father," or "Dad." And he understands us and loves us very much.

## THE HEART OF THE SERMON
## ON THE MOUNT
The[3] Gospel of Matthew places the text of the Lord's Prayer

strategically at the center of the Sermon on the Mount (cf. 6:9–13).

Now, let us observe the scene: Jesus goes up the hill by the lake, and sits down; he has his most intimate disciples circled around him, and then a large crowd of anonymous faces. It is this heterogeneous assembly that receives the consignment of the Our Father for the first time.

The location, as I said, is highly significant; because in this lengthy teaching, which falls under the title of Sermon on the Mount (cf. Mt 5:1—7:27), Jesus summarizes the fundamental aspects of his message. The beginning is like an archway decorated for a celebration: the Beatitudes. Jesus crowns with happiness a series of categories of people who in his time — but also in ours! — were not highly regarded. Blessed are the poor, the meek, the merciful, people humble of heart. ... This is the revolution of the Gospel. Where the Gospel is, there is revolution. The Gospel does not leave us calm, it drives us: it is revolutionary.

All people capable of love, the peacemakers who until now ended up at the margins of history, are instead the builders of the kingdom of God. It is as Jesus would say: go forth, you who bear in your heart the mystery of a God who has revealed his omnipotence in love and in forgiveness!

From this portal of entry, which overturns historical values, blooms the newness of the Gospel. The Law does not need to be abolished but needs a new interpretation that leads it back to its original meaning. If a person has a good heart, predisposed to love, then he understands that every word of God must be incarnated up to its ultimate results. Love has no boundaries: One can love one's spouse, one's friend, and even one's enemy with a wholly new perspective. Jesus says, "But I say to you, love your enemies, and pray for those who persecute you, so that you may be sons of your Father who is in heaven; for he makes his sun rise on the evil and on the good, and sends rain on the just and on the unjust" (Mt 5:44–45).

Here is the great secret underlying the whole Sermon on the Mount: *be children of your Father who is in heaven.* Apparently, these chapters of the Gospel of Matthew seem to be a moral discourse; they seem to evoke an ethic so demanding as to appear unfeasible, and instead we discover that they are above all a theological discourse. A Christian is not one who is committed to being better than others: He knows he is a sinner like everyone. A Christian is simply a person who pauses before the new Burning Bush, at the revelation of a God who does not bear the enigma of an unspeakable name, but asks his children to invoke him with the name of "Father," to allow themselves to be renewed by his power and to reflect a ray of his goodness for this world so thirsty for good, thus awaiting good news.

This is how Jesus introduces the teaching of the Our Father prayer. He does so by distancing himself from two groups of his time. First and foremost, hypocrites: "You must not be like the hypocrites; for they love to stand and pray in the synagogues and at the street corners, that they may be seen by men" (Mt 6:5). There are people who are able to compose atheistic prayers, without God, and they do so in order to be admired by people. And how often we see the scandal of those people who go to church and are there all day long, or go every day, and then live by hating others or speaking ill of people. This is a scandal! It is better not to go to church: living this way, as if they were atheists. But if you go to church, live as a child, as a brother or sister, and bear true witness, not a counter-witness. Christian prayer, however, has no other credible witness than one's own conscience, where one weaves a most intense dialogue with the Father: "When you pray, go into your room and shut the door and pray to your Father who is in secret" (6:6).

Then Jesus distances himself from the prayer of pagans: "Do not heap up empty phrases ... for they think that they will be heard for their many words" (v. 7). Here perhaps Jesus is alluding to that *captatio benevolentiae* that was the necessary introduction to many ancient prayers: divinity had to be in some way adapted from a long series of praises, of prayers, too. Let us consider that scene on Mount Carmel, when the Prophet Elijah challenged the priests of Baal. They shouted, danced, and asked for many things, that their god would listen to them. But Elijah instead remained silent, and the Lord revealed himself to Elijah. Pagans think that one prays by speaking, speaking, speaking, speaking. I also think of many Christians who think that praying is — pardon me — talking to God like parrots. No! One prays from the heart, from within. You, instead — Jesus says — when you pray, address God as a child to his father, who knows the things that are needed before he even asks him for them (cf. Mt 6:8). The Our Father could also be a silent prayer: It is essentially enough to place yourself under God's gaze, to remember his fatherly love, and this is all it takes to be satisfied.

It is beautiful to think that our God does not need sacrifices in order to win his favor! Our God needs nothing: In prayer, he only asks that we keep a channel of communication open with him in order to always recognize that we are his most beloved children. He loves us very much.

## KNOCK AND THE DOOR WILL BE OPENED TO YOU

Today's[4] catechesis refers to the Gospel of Luke. In fact, it is especially this Gospel, beginning with the childhood narratives, which describe the figure of Christ in an atmosphere dense with prayer. In it are the contents of three hymns which each day articulate the Church's prayer: the *Benedictus*, the *Magnificat*, and the *Nunc Dimittis*.

And we are moving forward in this catechesis on the Our Father; we see Jesus as a *prayerful* man. Jesus prays. In Luke's narrative, for example, the episode of the Transfiguration springs from a moment of prayer. It says this: "And as he was praying, the appearance of his countenance was altered, and his raiment became dazzling white" (9:29). But each step in Jesus' life is as if gently propelled by the breath of the Holy Spirit who guides him in every action. Jesus prays in the baptism on the Jordan; he dialogues with the Father before taking the most important decisions; he often withdraws in solitude to pray; he intercedes for Peter who will soon deny him. He says, "Simon, Simon, behold, Satan demanded to have you, that he might sift you like wheat, but I have prayed for you that your faith may not fail" (22:31–32). This is comforting: to know that Jesus prays for us, prays for me, for each one of us so that our faith will not fail. And this is true. "But

Father, does he still do so?" He still does so before the Father. "Jesus prays for me." Each one of us can say so. And we can also say to Jesus: "You are praying for me; continue to pray because I am in need of it." In this way: courageous.

Even the Messiah's death is immersed in a climate of prayer, such that the hours of the Passion seem characterized by a surprising calm: Jesus consoles the women, prays for his crucifiers, promises heaven to the good thief, and he breathes his last breath, saying, "Father, into thy hands I commit my spirit!" (23:46). Jesus' prayer seems to allay the most violent emotions, the desire for vendetta and revenge; it reconciles man with his fierce enemy, reconciles man with this enemy, which is death.

It is also in the Gospel of Luke that we find the request, expressed by one of the disciples, to be able to be taught to pray by Jesus himself. And it says this: "Lord, teach us to pray" (11:1). They saw him praying. "Teach us" — we too can say to the Lord — "Lord, you are praying for me, I know, but teach me how to pray so that I too can pray."

This request — "Lord, teach us to pray" — generates a rather lengthy lesson, through which Jesus explains to his followers with which words and which sentiments they must address God.

The first part of this lesson is precisely the Our Father. Pray thus: "Father, who art in heaven." "Father": that word which is so beautiful to say. We can always remain in prayer with that word alone: "Father." And to feel that we have a father: not a master nor a stepfather. No: a father. A Christian addresses God first of all by calling him "Father."

In this teaching that Jesus gives his disciples, it is interesting to pause on a few instructions that crown the text of the prayer. To give us confidence, Jesus explains several things. These focus on the attitudes of the believer who prays. For example, there is the parable of the importunate friend, who goes to disturb an entire family that is sleeping, because a person suddenly arrived from a journey, and he has no bread to offer him. What does Jesus say to this man who knocks on the door and wakes his friend? "I tell you" — Jesus explains — "though he will not get up and give him anything because he is his friend, yet because of his importunity he will rise and give him whatever he needs" (11:8). With this, he wants to teach us to pray and to persevere in prayer. And immediately afterward he gives the example of a father who has a hungry son. All of you, fathers and grandfathers who are here, when a son or grandson asks for something, is hungry, and asks and asks, then cries, shouts that he's hungry: "What father among you, if his son asks for a fish, will instead of a fish give him a serpent?" (v. 11). And all of you have experienced this: when the son asks, you give him what he wants to eat for his own good.

With these words Jesus makes it understood that God always responds, that no prayer will remain unheard. Why? Because he is Father and does not forget his suffering children.

Of course, these affirmations disconcert us, because many of our prayers seem not to obtain any results. How often have we asked and not received — we have all experienced this — how many times have we knocked and found a closed door? Jesus advises us, in those moments, to *persist and to not give up*. Prayer always transforms reality, always. If things around us do not change, at least we change; our heart changes. Jesus promised the gift of the Holy Spirit to each man and to each woman who prays.

We can be certain that God will respond. The only uncertainty is due to time, but let us not doubt that he will respond. Perhaps we will have to persist for our whole life, but he will respond. He promised us this: He is not like a father who gives a serpent instead of a fish. There is nothing more certain: the desire for happiness which we all carry in our heart will one day be fulfilled. Jesus asks: "Will God not vindicate his elect, who cry to him day and night?" (Lk 18:7). Yes, he will mete out justice; he will hear us. What a day of glory and resurrection that day will be! Henceforth, praying is victory over solitude and desperation. Praying. Prayer transforms reality; let us not forget this. It either changes things or changes our heart, but it always transforms. Henceforth, praying is victory over solitude and desperation. It is like seeing every fragment of creation teeming amid the listlessness of a history whose meaning we sometimes fail to grasp. But it is in motion, it is on a journey, and at the end of every road: What is there at the end of our road? At the end of prayer, at the end of the time in which we are praying, at life's end: What is there? There is a Father who awaits everything and everyone with arms wide open. Let us look to this Father.

### *ABBA*, FATHER!

In[5] the New Testament, the prayer seems to arrive at the essential, actually focusing on a single word: *Abba*, Father.

We have heard what Saint Paul writes in the Letter to the Romans: "You did not receive the spirit of slavery to fall back into fear, but you have received the spirit of sonship.

When we cry, '*Abba*, Father!'" (8:15). And the apostle says to the Galatians: "And because you are sons, God has sent the Spirit of his Son into our hearts, crying, 'Abba! Father!'" (Gal 4:6). The same invocation, in which all the novelty of the Gospel is condensed, recurs twice. After meeting Jesus and hearing his preaching, a Christian no longer considers God as a tyrant to be feared; he is no longer afraid but feels trust in him to expand in his heart: he can speak with the Creator by calling him "Father." The expression is so important for Christians that it is often preserved intact, in its original form: "*Abba*."

In the New Testament it is rare for Aramaic expressions to be translated into Greek. We have to imagine that the voice of Jesus himself has remained in these Aramaic words as if "recorded": They have respected Jesus' idiom. In the first words of the Our Father we immediately find the radical newness of Christian prayer.

It does not simply use a symbol — in this case, the father figure — to connect to the mystery of God; it is instead about having, so to speak, Jesus' entire world poured into one's heart. If we do this, we can truly pray the Our Father. Saying "*Abba*" is something much more intimate, more moving than simply calling God "Father." This is why someone has proposed translating this original Aramaic word "*Abba*" with "Dad" or "Papa." Instead of saying "our Father," saying "Dad, Papa." We shall continue to say "our Father," but with the heart we are invited to say "Dad," to have a relationship with God like that of a child with his dad, who says "Dad" and says "Papa." Indeed, these expressions evoke affection, they evoke warmth, something that casts us into the context of childhood: the image of a child completely enveloped in the embrace of a father who feels infinite tenderness for him. And for this reason, dear brothers and sisters, in order to pray properly, one must come to have a child's heart. Not a self-sufficient heart: one cannot pray properly this way. Like a child in the arms of his father, of his dad, of his papa.

But, of course, the Gospels better explain the meaning of this word. What does this word mean to Jesus? The Our Father takes on meaning and color if we learn to pray it after having read, for example, the parable of the merciful father in Chapter 15 of Luke (cf. vv. 11-32). Let us imagine this prayer recited by the prodigal son, after having experienced the embrace of his father who had long awaited him, a father who does not remember the offensive words the son had said to him, a father who now simply makes him understand how much he has been missed. Thus we discover how those words become vibrant, receive strength. And let us ask ourselves: Is it possible that you, O God, really know only love? Do you not know hatred? "No," God would respond, "I know only love."

"Where in you is vengeance, the demand for justice, anger at your wounded honor?" And God would respond, "I know only love."

In that parable the father's manner of conduct somehow recalls the spirit of a *mother*. It is especially mothers who excuse their children, who protect them, who do not suspend empathy for them, who continue to love them, even when they would no longer deserve anything.

It is enough to evoke this single expression — *Abba* — for Christian prayer to develop. And in his letters, Saint Paul follows this same path, because it is the path taught by Jesus: in this invocation there is a force that draws all the rest of the prayer.

God seeks you, even if you do not seek him. God loves you, even if you have forgotten about him. God glimpses beauty in you, even if you think you have squandered all your talents in vain. God is not only a father; he is like a mother who never stops loving her little child. On the other hand, there is a "gestation" that lasts forever, well beyond the nine months of the physical one; it is a gestation that engenders an infinite cycle of love.

For a Christian, praying is simply saying *"Abba"*; it is saying "Dad," saying "Papa," saying "Father," but with a child's trust.

It may be that we, too, happen to walk on paths far from God, as happened to the prodigal son; or to sink into a loneliness that makes us feel abandoned in the world; or even to make mistakes and be paralyzed by a sense of guilt. In those difficult moments, we can still find the strength to pray, to begin again with the word *"Abba,"* but said with the tender feeling of a child: *"Abba,"* "Dad." He does not hide his face from us. Remember well: perhaps one has bad things within, things he does not know how to resolve, much bitterness for having done this and that. ... He does not hide his face. He does not close himself off in silence. Say "Father" to him and he will answer you. You have a father. "Yes, but I am a delinquent ... " But you have a father who loves you! Say "Father" to him, start to pray in this way, and in the silence he will tell us that he has never lost sight of us. "But Father, I have done this ... " — "I have never lost sight of you; I have seen everything. But I have always been there, close to you, faithful to my love for you." That will be his answer. Never forget to say "Father."

## THE FATHER OF US ALL

Let[6] us continue our journey to learn ever better to pray as Jesus taught us. We must pray as he taught us to pray.

He said, "When you pray, go quietly into your room, withdraw from the world, and turn to God by calling him 'Father!'" Jesus does not want his disciples to be like the hypocrites who pray while standing in the squares to be admired by the people (cf. Mt 6:5). Jesus does not want hypocrisy. True prayer is that done in the secret of the conscience, of the heart: inscrutable, visible only to God. God and I. It shuns falsehood: With God it is impossible to pretend. It is impossible; there are no tricks that have any power before God. God knows us like this, naked in one's conscience, and there can be no pretense. At the root of the dialogue with God, there is a silent dialogue. Like the glance between two people in love: man's gaze meets God's, and this is prayer. Looking at God and allowing yourself to be looked upon by God: this is prayer. "But, Father, I do not say any words ... " Look at God and let yourself be looked upon by him: it is a prayer, a beautiful prayer!

Yet, although the disciple's prayer may be completely confidential, it is never lacking in intimacy. In the secret of the conscience, a Christian does not leave the world outside the door of his room, but carries people and situations, the problems, many things in his heart; I bring them all to prayer.

There is a striking absence in the text of the Lord's Prayer.

Were I to ask you what the striking absence in the text of the Lord's Prayer is, it would not be easy to answer. A word is missing. Everyone think: What is missing from the Lord's Prayer? Think, what is missing? One word. One word which in our times — perhaps always — everyone holds in great consideration. What is the missing word in the Lord's Prayer that we pray every day? To save time, I will tell you: the word "I" is missing. "I" is never said. Jesus teaches us to pray with "*you*" on our lips, because Christian prayer is a dialogue: "blessed be *your* name, *your* kingdom come, *your* will be done." Not *my* name, *my* kingdom, *my* will. Not *I*, it is no good. And then it moves on to *we*. The entire second part of the Our Father uses the first person plural: "*give us our* daily bread, forgive *us our* sins, lead *us* not into temptation, deliver *us* from evil." Even the most basic of man's requests — such as that of having food to satisfy hunger — are all in the plural. In Christian prayer, no one asks for bread for themselves: *give me* bread today — no, *give us*, it is asked for all, for all the world's poor. We must not forget this. The word I is missing. We pray by using you and we. It is a good lesson from Jesus. Do not forget this.

Why? Why is there no room for individualism in the dialogue with God? There is no display of our own problems, as if we were the only ones suffering in the world. There is no prayer raised to God that is not the prayer of a *community of brothers and sisters*. "We": we are a community; we are brothers and sisters; we are a people who pray: "we." Once, a prison chaplain asked me a question: "Tell me Father, what is the opposite of I?" And naively, I said, "you." "This is the start of war. The opposite of I is us, where there is peace, all are together." I received a beautiful lesson from that priest.

In prayer, a Christian bears all the difficulties of the people who live beside him: When night falls, he tells God about the suffering he has come across that day; he sets before him many faces, friends, and even those who are hostile; he does not shoo them away as dangerous distractions. If you do not realize that there are many people suffering around you, if you are not moved by the tears of the poor, if you are accustomed to everything, then it means your heart ... what is it like? Withered? No, worse: It is made of stone. In this case it is good to implore the Lord to touch us with his Spirit and soften our heart: "Soften my heart, Lord." It is a beautiful prayer: "Lord, soften my heart, so that I may understand and take on all the problems and all the suffering of others." Christ did not pass unscathed beside the miseries of the world: each time he perceived loneliness, physical or spiritual pain, he felt a strong sense of compassion, like a mother's womb. This "feeling compassion" — let us not forget this word that is so Christian: "feeling compassion" — is one of the key words of the Gospel: It is what inspires the Good Samaritan to approach the wounded man by the roadside, unlike others who are hard of heart.

We can ask ourselves: When I pray, am I open to the cries of many people near and far? Or do I think of prayer as a type of anesthesia, in order to be more at peace? I am just tossing the question out there, each of you can answer to yourself. In such case I would be the victim of a terrible misunderstanding. Of course, mine would no longer be a Christian prayer. Because that we that Jesus taught us prevents me from being at peace by myself and makes me feel responsible for my brothers and sisters.

There are people who seemingly do not seek God, but Jesus asks us to pray for them, too, because God seeks these people more than anyone else. Jesus did not come for the healthy, but for the sick, for sinners (cf. Lk 5:31) — that is, for everyone, because whoever thinks he is healthy, in reality is not. If we work for justice, we do not feel we are better than others: The Father makes the sun rise on the good and on the evil (cf. Mt 5:45). The Father loves everyone! Let us learn from God who is always good to everyone, opposite to us, who are able to be good only to certain people, with someone I like.

Brothers and sisters, saints and sinners, we are all brothers and sisters loved by the same Father. And, in the evening of life, we will be judged on love, on how we have loved. Not merely sentimental love, but compassionate and tangible love, according to the Gospel rule —do not forget it! — "As you did it to one of the least of these my brethren, you did it to me" (Mt 25:40). So says the Lord. Thank you.

## WHO ART IN HEAVEN

The[7] first step of every Christian prayer is the entry into a mystery, that of the *fatherhood of God*. One cannot pray like parrots. Either you enter into the mystery, in the awareness that God is your Father, or you do not pray. If I want to pray to God my Father, I begin with the mystery. To understand to what measure God is father to us, let us consider the figures of our parents, but in some measure we must always "refine them," purify them. The *Catechism of the Catholic Church* also says so ... : "The purification of our hearts has to do with paternal or maternal images, stemming from our personal and cultural history, and influencing our relationship with God" (2779).

None of us has had perfect parents, no one; as we, in turn, will never be perfect parents or pastors. We all have shortcomings, everyone. We always experience our loving relationships according to our limitations and also our egotism; thus they are often tarnished by desires to possess or to manipulate others. For this reason, at times declarations of love are transformed into feelings of anger and hostility. But look, last week these two loved each other so much; today they hate each other to death: We see this every day! This is why we all have, within, bitter roots that are not good, and sometimes they come out and do harm.

For this reason, when we speak of God as father, as we consider the image of our parents, especially if they loved us, at the same time we must go further. Because God's love is that of the Father *who art in heaven*, according to the expression that Jesus invites us to use: he is the total love that we can savor only imperfectly in this life. ...

The expression "in heaven" is not intended to express a distance, but rather a radical difference of love, another dimension of love, a tireless love, a love that will always be there, that is always at hand. It is enough to say, "Our Father who art in heaven," and that love comes.

Therefore, have no fear. None of us is alone. If even by misfortune your earthly father were to forget you and you were resentful of him, you are not denied the fundamental experience of Christian faith: knowing that you are a *most deeply beloved son or daughter of God*, and that there is nothing in life that can extinguish his heartfelt love for you.

## PRAYER DRIVES AWAY ALL FEAR

In[8] our journey of rediscovering the Our Father, today we shall delve deeper into the first of his seven invocations — namely, "hallowed be thy name."

There are seven requests in the Our Father, easily divisible into two subgroups. The first three have at the center "thou/you" addressed to God the Father; the other four have at the center "us" and our human needs. In the first part Jesus lets us enter his wishes, everyone turning to the Father: "hallowed by *thy* name, *thy* kingdom come, *thy* will be done"; in the second it is he who enters us and becomes the interpreter of *our* needs: daily bread, forgiveness of sins, help in temptation, and liberation from evil.

Herein lies the matrix of every Christian prayer — I would say of every human prayer — which is always done, on the one hand, as a *contemplation* of God, of his mystery, of his beauty and goodness, and on the other, as a sincere and courageous *request* for what we need for life, and to live properly. Thus, in its simplicity and in its essentiality, the Our Father teaches those who pray it not to multiply empty words, because — as Jesus himself says — "your Father knows what you need before you ask him" (Mt 6:8).

When we speak with God, we do not do so in order to reveal what we have in our heart: He knows it much better than we do! Although God is a mystery for us, we are not an enigma in his eyes (cf. Ps 139:1-4). God is like those mothers for whom one look suffices to thoroughly understand her children: whether they are happy or sad, whether they are sincere or are hiding something. ...

Thus the first step in Christian prayer is consigning ourselves to God, to his providence. It is as if to say: "Lord, you know everything; I do not even have to tell you about my pain; I ask only that you be here beside me: You are my hope." It is interesting to note that, in the Sermon on the Mount, immediately after teaching the words of the Our Father, Jesus exhorts us not to be worried or troubled about things. It seems like a contradiction: First he teaches us to ask for daily bread, and then he tells us: "Do not be anxious, asking 'What shall we eat?' or 'What shall we drink?' or 'What shall we wear?'" (Mt 6:31). But the contradiction is only apparent: A Christian's request expresses trust in the Father, and it is precisely this trust that enables us to ask for what we need without worry or agitation.

This is why we pray by saying, *"Hallowed be thy name!"* In this request — the first one! *"Hallowed be thy name!* — one feels all Jesus' admiration for the beauty and greatness of the Father, and the wish that everyone recognize and love him for what he truly is. And at the same time there is the supplication that his name be sanctified in us, in our family, in our community, in the entire world. It is God who sanctifies, who transforms us with his love, but at the same time we too, with our witness, manifest God's holiness in the world, making his name present. God is holy, but if we, if our life is not holy, there is great inconsistency! God's holiness must be reflected in our actions, in our life. "I am Christian; God is holy, but I do many bad things": no, this is of no use. This also does harm; this scandalizes and does not help.

God's holiness is an expanding force, and we ask that the barriers in our world be quickly broken down. When Jesus begins to preach, the first to pay the consequences is precisely the evil that afflicts the world. The evil spirits curse: "What have you to do with us, Jesus of Nazareth? Have you come to destroy us? I know who you are, the Holy One of God" (Mk 1:24). Such holiness had never been seen before: not concerned with itself but radiating outward. A holiness — that of Jesus — that expands in concentric circles, as when one throws a stone into a pond. The evil one's days are numbered — evil is not eternal; evil can no longer harm us: the strong man has arrived to take possession of his house (cf. Mk 3:23-27). And this strong man is Jesus, who gives us, too, the strength to take possession of our inner house.

Prayer drives away all fears. The Father loves us; the Son lifts up his arms to support ours; the Spirit works secretly for the redemption of the world. And we? We do not waver in uncertainty; for we have one great certainty: God loves me; Jesus gave his life for me! The Spirit is within me. This is the great certainty. And the evil one? He is afraid. And this is good.

## THY KINGDOM COME

When[9] we pray the Our Father, the second request we address to God is, "Thy kingdom come" (Mt 6:10). After praying for the sanctification of his name, the believer expresses the desire that his kingdom may come soon. This desire poured forth, so to speak, from the very heart of Christ who began preaching in Galilee by proclaiming, "The time is fulfilled, and the kingdom of God is at hand; repent, and believe in the gospel" (Mk 1:15). These words are in no way a threat. On the contrary, they are a blessed proclamation, a joyful message. Jesus does not want to press people to convert by sowing fear of God's imminent judgment or a sense of guilt for the wrongdoing committed. Jesus does not proselytize: he simply proclaims. Rather, what he brings is the Good News of salvation, and, starting from this, he calls us to convert. Each of us is invited to believe in the Gospel: God's authority is brought close to his children. This is the Gospel: the authority of God drawn near to his children. And Jesus announces this marvelous thing, this grace: God, the Father, loves us, is close to us, and teaches us to walk on the path of holiness.

The signs of the coming of this kingdom are multiple, all of them positive. Jesus begins his ministry by caring for the sick, both in body and in spirit, for those who were socially excluded — lepers, for example — and sinners who were looked upon with scorn by everyone, even by those who were greater sinners than them but who pretended to be just. And what does Jesus call them? Hypocrites. Jesus himself indicates these signs, the signs of the kingdom of God: "The blind receive their sight and the lame walk, lepers are cleansed and the deaf hear, and the dead are raised up, and the poor have good news preached to them" (Mt 11:5).

"Thy kingdom come" Christians persistently repeat when they pray the Our Father. Jesus has come; but the world is still marked by sin, inhabited by many people who suffer, by people who do not want to reconcile and do not forgive, by war and many forms of exploitation. Let us think about child trafficking, for example. All these facts are proof that Christ's victory has not yet been completely attained. Many men and women still live with closed hearts. It is above all in these situations that the second request of the Our Father emerges on the lips of Christians: "Thy kingdom come!", which is like saying: "We need you, Father! We need you, Jesus. We need you, Lord, to be everywhere and for ever, in our midst!" Thy kingdom come, may you be in our midst.

We sometimes ask ourselves: why is this kingdom so slow to come about? Jesus likes to speak of his victory in terms of parables. For example, he says that the kingdom of God is similar to a field where weeds and good wheat grow together: the biggest mistake would be to immediately intervene, by uprooting from the world what appear to us to be invasive weeds. God is not like us. God is patient. It is not through violence that the kingdom is established in the world: meekness is its means of propagation (cf. Mt 13:24–30).

The kingdom of God is certainly a great strength, the greatest one there is, but not according to worldly criteria. This is why it never appears to have the absolute majority. It is like leaven that is kneaded with flour: it apparently disappears, and yet it is what makes the dough rise (cf. Mt 13:33). Or it is like a mustard seed, so small, almost invisible, which, however, carries within it nature's most explosive force, and once fully grown it becomes the largest tree in the garden (cf. Mt 13:31–32).

In this "destiny" of the kingdom of God, we can sense the tenor of Jesus' life. He too was a frail sign to his contemporaries, an almost unknown event to the official historians of the time. He described himself as a "grain of wheat" that dies in the earth, but only in this way can it bear "much fruit" (cf. Jn 12:24). The symbol of the seed is eloquent. One day a farmer plants it in the earth (a gesture which resembles a burial), and then, if he "should sleep and rise night and day, and the seed should sprout and grow, he knows not how"

(Mk 4:27). A seed that sprouts is more the work of God than of the man who planted it (cf. Mk 4:27). God always precedes us. God always surprises. Thanks to him, the night of Good Friday is followed by the dawn of the Resurrection, able to illuminate the entire world with hope.

"Thy kingdom come!" Let us sow this word in the midst of our sins and our shortcomings. Let us give it to the people defeated and bent by life, to those who have tasted hatred more than love, those who have lived aimless days without ever understanding why. Let us give it to those who have fought for justice, to all the martyrs in history, to those who have come to the conclusion that they have fought for nothing and that in this world evil always dominates. We will then feel the prayer of the Our Father respond. It will repeat those words of hope for the umpteenth time, the same words with which the Spirit sealed all the Sacred Scriptures: "Yes, I am coming soon." This is the Lord's reply: "I am coming soon." Amen. And the Lord's Church responds: "Come, Lord, Jesus" (cf. Acts 2:20). "Thy kingdom come" is like saying "Come, Lord, Jesus." And Jesus says, "I am coming soon." And Jesus comes in his way, but every day. We have trust in this. And when we pray the Our Father, we always say, "Thy kingdom come," in order to feel him say in our heart, "Yes, yes, I am coming, and I am coming soon."

## THY WILL BE DONE
Continuing[10] our catechesis on the Lord's Prayer, today we will pause on the third invocation: "Thy will be done." It should be read together with the first two — "hallowed be thy name" and "thy kingdom come" — so that they jointly form

a triptych: "hallowed be thy name," "thy kingdom come," "thy will be done." Today we will speak about the third.

Before man's care for the world, there is the tireless care God employs for man and for the world. The whole Gospel reflects this inversion of perspective. The sinner Zacchaeus climbs up a tree because he wants to see Jesus, but he does not know that, much earlier, God had sought him. When Jesus arrives, he says to him: "Zacchaeus, make haste and come down; for I must stay at your house today." And at the end he states: "The Son of man came to seek and to save the lost" (Lk 19:5-10). This is *God's will*, what we pray to be done. What is God's will, incarnated in Jesus? To seek and to save the one who is lost. And in prayer, we ask that God's seeking may be successful, that his universal plan of salvation may be accomplished, first in each of us, and then in the entire world. Have you thought about what it means that God seeks me? Each one of us can say: "But does God seek me?" — "Yes! He seeks you! He seeks me": He seeks each one of us, personally. But God is great! How much love there is behind all this.

God is not ambiguous. He never conceals himself behind enigmas. He did not plan the world's future in an incomprehensible way. No. He is clear. If we do not understand this, then we also risk not understanding the meaning of the third expression of the Our Father. Indeed, the Bible is filled with expressions that tell us about God's positive will for the world. And in the *Catechism of the Catholic Church,* we find a collection of quotes that bear witness to this faithful and patient divine will (cf. 2821-27). And in his First Letter to Timothy, Saint Paul writes [that] God "desires all men to be saved and to come to the knowledge of the truth" (2:4). This, without a shadow of a doubt, is God's will: the salvation of man, of mankind, of each of us. God knocks upon the door of our heart with his love. Why? To attract us, to attract us to him, and to carry us forward on the path of salvation. God is close to each of us, with his love, to lead us by the hand to salvation. How much love there is behind this!

Therefore, by praying "thy will be done," we are not called to subserviently bow our head as if we were slaves. No! God wants us to be free; his love frees us. Indeed, the Our Father is the prayer of children, not of slaves; but of children who know their father's heart and are certain of his loving plan. Woe to us if, in uttering these words, we should shrug our shoulders as a sign of surrender to a destiny we find repellant and that we are unable to change. On the contrary, it is a prayer that is filled with ardent trust in God who wants good, life, and salvation for us. A courageous, even militant prayer, because there are many, too many realities in the world that are not in accordance with God's plan. We all know them. Paraphrasing the prophet Isaiah, we could say: "Here, Father, there is war, abuse of power, exploitation; but we know that you want our good. You want our good, therefore we implore you: thy will be done! Lord, overturn the world's plans, transform swords into plowshares and spears into pruning hooks: so that no one may learn the art of war anymore" (cf. 2:4). God wants peace.

The Our Father is a prayer which kindles in us the same love as Jesus' love for the Father's will, a flame that spurs us to transform the world with love. The Christian does not believe in an inescapable "fate." There is nothing unplanned in

Christian faith. Rather, there is a salvation waiting to manifest itself in the life of each man and woman, and to be fulfilled in eternity. When we pray, we believe that God can and wants to transform reality by overcoming evil with good. It makes sense to obey and to surrender oneself to this God, even at the hour of the most difficult trial.

So it was for Jesus in the Garden of Gethsemane when he experienced anguish and prayed: "Father, if thou art willing, remove this cup from me; nevertheless not my will, but thine, be done" (Lk 22:42). Jesus is crushed by the evil of the world. However, he trustingly surrenders himself to the ocean of love of the Father's will. The martyrs, too, were not seeking death in their trials. They were seeking the after-death, the resurrection. Out of love, God can lead us to walk along difficult paths and to experience wounds and painful thorns, but he will never forsake us. He will always be with us, beside us, within us. For a believer this is more than a hope, it is a certainty: God is with me. The same that we find in the parable in Luke's Gospel regarding the need to always pray. Jesus says: "Will not God vindicate his elect, who cry to him day and night? Will he delay long over them? I tell you, he will vindicate them speedily" (18:7–8). Such is the Lord. This is how he loves us.

## GIVE US OUR DAILY BREAD

Today[11] we move on to analyze the second part of the Lord's Prayer, in which we present our needs to God. This second part begins with a word with the scent of daily life: *bread*.

Jesus' prayer begins with a compelling request, which quite resembles a beggar's plea: "Give us our daily bread!"

This prayer comes from an evident [fact] that we often forget, which is to say that we are not self-sufficient beings, and that we need to nourish ourselves every day.

Scripture shows us that for many people the encounter with Jesus is realized by beginning with a request. Jesus does not ask for refined invocations, but rather the whole of human existence, with its most concrete and mundane problems, can become prayer. In the Gospels we find a multitude of mendicants who plead for liberation and salvation. Those who ask for bread, those for healing; some for purification, others sight; or that a dear one may live again. ... Jesus never moves indifferently past these requests and this suffering.

Thus Jesus teaches us to ask the Father for our daily bread. And he teaches us to do so united with many men and women for whom this prayer is a plea — often stifled within — which accompanies the anxiety of each day. How many mothers and how many fathers, even today, go to sleep with the torment of not having enough bread for their own children tomorrow! Let us imagine this prayer recited not in the security of a comfortable apartment, but in the precariousness of a room in which one adapts, where life's necessities are lacking. Jesus' words take on new meaning. Christian prayer begins at this level. It is not an exercise for ascetics; it begins from reality, from the heart and from the flesh of people who live in need, or who share the condition of those who do not have life's necessities. Not even the most exalted Christian mystics can overlook the simplicity of this request. "Father let there be the necessary bread for us and for all." And bread also means water, medicine, home, work. ... Asking for life's necessities.

The bread a Christian requests in prayer is not *mine*, but *ours*. This is what Jesus wants. He teaches us to request it not only for ourselves but for the world's entire fraternity. If one does not pray in this way, the Our Father ceases to be a Christian prayer. If God is our Father, how can we present ourselves to him without taking each other by the hand? All of us. And if we steal from one another the bread that he gives us, how can we call ourselves his children? This prayer contains an attitude of empathy, an attitude of solidarity. In my hunger I feel the hunger of the multitudes, and thus I will pray to God until their request is answered. This is how Jesus teaches his community, his Church, to bring to God the needs of all: "We are all your children, O Father, have mercy on us!" And now it will do us good to pause a bit and think about the starving children. Let us think about the children who are in warring countries: the starving children of Yemen, the starving children in Syria, the starving children in so many countries where there is no bread, in South Sudan. Let us think about these children and, thinking of them, let us recite the prayer together aloud, "Father, give us this day our daily bread." Everyone together.

## FORGIVE US OUR TRESPASSES
After[12] asking God for our daily bread, the Lord's Prayer enters the sphere of our relationships with others. Jesus teaches us to ask the Father: "Forgive us our debts, as we also have forgiven our debtors" (Mt 6:12). Just as we need bread, we also need forgiveness; this too, this every day.

A Christian who prays asks God first of all that his *debts* be forgiven — that is, his sins, the bad things he does. This is the first truth of every prayer: Even if we were perfect people, even if we were pure saints who never deviate from a virtuous life, we continue to be children who owe everything to the Father. What is the most dangerous attitude for every Christian life? It is pride. It is the attitude of those who stand before God thinking that they always have their affairs in order with him: The proud think they have everything in order. Like that Pharisee in the parable who thinks he is praying in the Temple, but, in reality, he is commending himself before God: "I thank you, Lord, because I am not like the others." And the people who feel they are perfect, the people who criticize others, are proud people. None of us is perfect, no one. On the contrary, the tax collector, who was at the back of the Temple, a sinner despised by everyone, stops at the threshold of the Temple and does not feel worthy to enter and entrusts himself to God's mercy. And Jesus comments: "This man went down to his house justified rather than the other" (Lk 18:14) — that is, forgiven, saved. Why? Because he was not proud, because he recognized his limitations and his sins.

## AS WE FORGIVE THOSE WHO TRESPASS AGAINST US

In[13] the Church there is no *self-made man*, men who have created themselves. We are all debtors to God, and to all those people who have given us favorable living conditions. Our identity is built first and foremost with the good received. The first is life.

One who prays learns to say "thank you." And so often we forget to say thank you. We are selfish. One who prays learns to say thank you and to ask God to be benevolent to him or her. As much as we may strive, there is always an inexhaustible debt to God which we can never pay back: He loves us infinitely more than we love him. And then, as much as we try to live according to Christian teaching, in our life there will always be something for which to ask forgiveness. Let us think about days spent lazily, about moments in which rancor has filled our heart, and so on. These unfortunately not rare experiences are what make us implore: "Lord, Father, forgive us our debts." Thus we ask God for forgiveness. ...

The good God invites all of us to be good. The two parts of the invocation are linked together with a stern conjunction: We ask the Lord to forgive our debts, our sins, *as* we forgive our friends, the people who live with us, our neighbors, the people who have done something bad to us.

Every Christian knows that forgiveness of sins exists for him or her. We all know this: God forgives everything and forgives always. ... But the grace of God, so abundant, is always demanding. Those who have received much must learn to give much, and not to keep only for themselves what they have received. Those who have received much must learn to give much. It is not by chance that the Gospel of Matthew, immediately after having given the text of the Our Father, of the seven expressions used, pauses to emphasize precisely that of fraternal forgiveness: "For if you forgive men their trespasses, your heavenly Father also will forgive you; but if you do not forgive men their trespasses, neither will your Father forgive your trespasses" (6:14–15). But this is powerful! I recall: Several times I have heard people say: "I will never forgive that person! I will never forgive that person for what he did to me!" But if you do not forgive, God will not forgive you. You close the door. Let us consider whether we are able to forgive or if we do not forgive.

When I was in the other diocese, a distressed priest told me that he had gone to administer the last rites to an elderly woman who was on her deathbed. The poor woman could not speak. And the priest asked her: "Madam, do you repent of your sins?" The woman said "yes"; she could not confess them, but she said yes. It is sufficient. And then again: "Do you forgive others?" And the woman said, on her deathbed, "No." The priest was upset. If you do not forgive, God will not forgive you. Let us consider, we who are here, whether we forgive or whether we are able to forgive. "Father, I cannot do it, because those people treated me so harshly." But if you cannot do it, ask the Lord to give you the strength to do so: Lord, help me to forgive.

Here again, we find the connection between love of God and love of neighbor. Love attracts love; forgiveness attracts forgiveness. ... Let us consider today, in this most beautiful week of Easter, whether I am able to forgive. And if I do not feel I can, I must ask the Lord to give me the grace to forgive, because knowing how to forgive is a grace.

God gives every Christian the grace to write a story of good in the life of his or her brothers and sisters, especially of those who have done something regrettable or wrong. With a word, an embrace, a smile, we can pass on to others the most precious thing we have received. What is the most precious thing we have received? Forgiveness, which we too must be able to give to others.

## LEAD US NOT INTO TEMPTATION

"Lead[14] us not into temptation, but deliver us from evil" (Mt 6:13). Another version says, "Let us not fall into temptation." The Our Father begins in a calm manner: It makes us desire that God's great plan be fulfilled in our midst. It then casts a gaze on life and makes us ask ourselves what we need each day: daily bread. Then the prayer turns to our interpersonal relationships, often tarnished by selfishness: We request forgiveness, and we commit to bestow it. But it is with this penultimate invocation that our dialogue with the heavenly Father gets, so to speak, to the heart of the drama — that is, to the matter of the contrast between our freedom and the pitfalls of evil.

As we know, the original Greek expression contained in the Gospels is difficult to render in an exact manner, and all the modern translations are somewhat weak. But we can agree unanimously on one element: However one understands the text, we have to exclude the possibility that God is the protagonist of the temptations that loom over mankind's journey. ...

If anything, it is the contrary: The Father is not the creator of evil. He does not give a serpent to any child who asks for a fish (cf. Lk 11:11) — as Jesus teaches — and when evil appears in people's lives, he fights beside them, so they may be freed from it. A God who always fights for us, not against us. He is the Father! It is in this sense that we pray the Our Father. ...

In the most awful moments of our life, in the most painful moments, in the most anguishing moments, God watches with us; God fights alongside us; he is always close to us.

Why? Because he is Father. Thus we began the prayer: "Our Father." And a father does not abandon his children. That night of Jesus' suffering and struggle is the ultimate seal of the Incarnation: God descends to find us in our abyss and in the anguish that pervades our history. ...

Deliver us, thus, Oh God, from the time of trial and temptation. But when this time arrives for us, Our Father, show us that we are not alone. You are the Father. Show us that Christ has already taken upon himself the weight of that cross too. Show us that Jesus calls us to carry it with him, abandoning ourselves trustfully to your Fatherly love.

## BUT DELIVER US FROM EVIL

We[15] have finally reached the seventh request in the Our Father: "And lead us not into temptation" (Mt 6:13b).

With this expression, the one praying is not only asking not to be abandoned in times of temptation, but is also imploring to be delivered from evil. The original Greek verb is very powerful: It evokes the presence of the evil one who tends to grab hold of us and bite us (cf. 1 Pt 5:8) and from whom we ask God for deliverance. The apostle Peter also says that the evil one, the Devil, prowls around us like a roaring lion, to devour us, and we ask God to deliver us.

With this twofold plea — "Do not abandon us" and "deliver us" — an essential characteristic of Christian prayer emerges. Jesus teaches his friends to place the invocation of the Father above all else, also and especially in moments in which the evil one makes his threatening presence felt. Indeed, Christian prayer does not close its eyes to life. It is a filial prayer and not a childish prayer. It is not so infatuated with God's paternity as to forget that mankind's journey is filled with difficulties. If the last verses of the Our Father were not there, how could sinners, the persecuted, the desperate, the dying, pray? The last petition is precisely the petition we make when we are at the limit, always.

There is an evil in our lives that is an unassailable presence. ...

The prayerful are not blind and can clearly see before their eyes this evil that is so cumbersome, and so contradictory to God's mercy itself. They perceive it in nature, in history, even in their own heart. Because there are none among us who can say they are exempt from evil or, at least, that they have not been tempted by it. We all know what evil is; we all know what temptation is; we have all experienced temptation of some kind in the flesh. But it is the tempter who persuades and pushes us towards evil, telling us: "Do this, think about this, go down that road."

The last cry of the Our Father is cast against this "wide-brimmed" evil which keeps the most varied experiences under its umbrella: mankind's mourning, innocent suffering, slavery, the exploitation of others, the tears of innocent children. All these things protest in man's heart and become a voice in the final words of Jesus' prayer.

It is precisely in the narratives of the Passion that some expressions of the Our Father find their most striking resonance. Jesus says, "Abba, Father, all things are possible to thee: remove this cup from me; yet not what I will, but what thou wilt" (Mk 14:36). ...

Dear brothers and sisters, in this way, the Our Father is similar to a symphony which seeks to be fulfilled in each of us. A Christian knows how enslaving the power of evil is, and at the same time experiences how Jesus, who never gave in to its seduction, is on our side and comes to our aid.

Thus Jesus' prayer leaves us the most precious legacy: the presence of the Son of God who delivered us from evil, fighting to convert it. In the hour of the final struggle he commands Peter to put his sword back in its sheath; he ensures paradise to the thief; to all the people who were there, unaware of the tragedy that was taking place, he offers a word of peace: "Father, forgive them; for they know not what they do" (Lk 23:34).

From Jesus' forgiveness on the cross springs peace; true peace comes from the cross. It is the gift of the Risen One, a gift that Jesus gives us. Just think that the first greeting the risen Jesus gives is "peace be with you," peace in your souls, in your hearts, in your lives. The Lord gives us peace; he gives us forgiveness, but we must ask: "deliver us from evil," in order not to succumb to evil. This is our hope, the strength given to us by the Risen One who is in our midst: he is here. He is here with that strength that he gives us to go forward, and he promises to deliver us from evil.

## WHEREVER YOU ARE, CALL UPON THE FATHER

We[16] can say that Christian prayer arises from the courage to address God with the name "Father." This to say "Father" to God. But it takes courage! It is not so much a matter of a formula as much as a filial intimacy into which we are introduced by grace: Jesus is the revealer of the Father, and he gives us intimacy with him. He "does not give us a formula to repeat mechanically. As in every vocal prayer, it is through the word of God that the Holy Spirit teaches the children of God to pray to their Father" (*Catechism of the Catholic Church*, 2766). Jesus himself used different expressions to pray to the Father. If we read the Gospels carefully, we discover that these expressions of prayer that come from Jesus' lips recall the text of the Our Father.

For example, on the night of Gethsemane, Jesus prays this way: "Abba, Father, all things are possible to thee; remove this cup from me; yet not what I will, but what thou wilt" (Mk 14:36). We have already cited this text from Mark's Gospel. How can we fail to recognize in this prayer, albeit short, a trace of the Our Father? In the midst of darkness, Jesus invokes God with the name "Abba," with filial trust and, despite feeling fear and anguish, he asks that his will be done.

In other passages of the Gospel, Jesus insists that his disciples nurture a spirit of prayer. Prayer must be insistent, and above all it must carry the memory of our brothers and sisters, especially when we have difficult relationships with them. Jesus says, "Whenever you stand praying, forgive, if you have anything against any one; so that your Father also who is in heaven may forgive you your trespasses" (Mk 11:25). How can we fail to recognize in these expressions, their consonance with the Our Father? And the examples could be numerous, also for us.

We do not find the Our Father in Saint Paul's writings, but its presence emerges in that wonderful summary where the invocation of the Christian is condensed into a single word: "Abba!" (cf. Rom 8:15; Gal 4:6).

In Luke's Gospel, Jesus fully satisfies the request of the disciples who, seeing him withdraw and immerse himself in prayer, decide to ask him one day, "Lord, teach us to pray, as John [the Baptist] taught his disciples" (Lk 11:1). And so the Teacher taught them to pray to the Father.

When considering the New Testament as a whole, one can clearly see that the first protagonist of every Christian prayer is the Holy Spirit. But let us not forget this: The protagonist of every Christian prayer is the Holy Spirit. We could never pray without the power of the Holy Spirit. It is he who prays within us and moves us to pray well. We can ask the Holy Spirit to teach us to pray because he is the protagonist, the one who makes the true prayer within us. He breathes into the heart of each of us who are Jesus' disciples. The Holy Spirit makes us able to pray as children of God, as we truly are by our baptism. The Holy Spirit helps us pray in the "furrow" that Jesus ploughed for us. This is the mystery of Christian prayer: By grace we are attracted to that dialogue of love of the most Holy Trinity.

Jesus prayed this way. At times he used expressions that are certainly far removed from the text of the Our Father. Let us think about the initial words of Psalm 22 that Jesus uttered on the cross: "My God, my God, why hast thou forsaken me?" (Mt 27:46). Can the heavenly Father abandon his Son? Certainly not. And yet, his love for us, sinners, brought Jesus to this point: up to experiencing the abandonment of God, his distance, because he took our sins upon himself. But even in his anguished cry, "*my* God, *my* God" remains. In that "my" lies the core of the relationship with the Father; there lies the core of faith and of prayer.

This is why, starting from this core, a Christian can pray in any situation. He can adopt all the prayers of the Bible, especially of the Psalms; but he can also pray with many expressions that in thousands of years of history have gushed forth from the heart of mankind. And let us never cease to tell the Father about our brothers and sisters in humanity, so that none of them, particularly the poor, may remain without comfort or a portion of love.

At the end of this catechesis, we can repeat that prayer of Jesus: "I thank thee, Father, Lord of heaven and earth, that thou hast hidden these things from the wise and understanding and revealed them to babes" (Lk 10:21). In order to pray, we have to make ourselves little so that the Holy Spirit may come within us and may be the One to lead us in prayer.

# A TRANSFORMING ENCOUNTER

## WELLSPRING OF MERCY

The[1] Gospel parable which we have just listened to (cf. Lk 18:1–8) contains an important teaching: We ought "always to pray and not lose heart" (v. 1). This means, then, pray constantly, not just when I feel like it. No, Jesus says that we ought "always to pray and not lose heart." And he offers the example of the widow and the judge.

The judge is a powerful person, called to issue judgment on the basis of the Law of Moses. That is why the biblical tradition recommended that judges be people who fear God, who are worthy of faith, impartial, and incorruptible (cf. Ex 18:21). However, this judge "neither feared God nor regarded man" (Lk 18:2). As a judge, he was unfair, unscrupulous, who did not take the Law into account but did whatever he wanted, according to his own interests. It was to him that a widow turned for justice. Widows, along with orphans and foreigners, were the most vulnerable groups of society. The rights afforded them by the Law could be easily disregarded because, being isolated and defenseless, they could hardly be assertive. A poor widow, alone, with no one to defend her, might be ignored, might even be denied justice. Just as the orphan, just as the foreigner, the migrant: in that time this was a very serious problem. Faced with the judge's indifference, the widow has recourse to her only weapon: to bother him incessantly with her request for justice. And because of her insistence, she achieves her end. At a certain point, the judge grants her request, not because he is moved by mercy or because his conscience has been working on him; he simply admits, "Because this widow bothers me, I will vindicate her, or she will wear me out by her continual coming" (v. 5).

From this parable Jesus draws two conclusions: If the widow could manage to bend the dishonest judge with her incessant requests, how much more will God, who is the good and just Father, "vindicate his elect, who cry to him day and night"; moreover, will not "delay long over them," but will act "speedily" (vv. 7-8).

That is why Jesus urges us to pray and "not to lose heart." We all go through times of tiredness and discouragement, especially when our prayers seem ineffective. But Jesus assures us: Unlike the dishonest judge, God promptly answers his children, even though this doesn't mean he will necessarily do it when and how we would like. Prayer does not work like a magic wand! It helps us keep faith in God, and to entrust ourselves to him even when we do not understand his will. In this, Jesus himself — who prayed constantly! — is our model. The Letter to the Hebrews reminds us, "In the days of his flesh, Jesus offered up prayers and supplications, with loud cries and tears, to him [God] who was able to save him from death, and he was heard for his godly fear" (5:7). At first glance this statement seems far-fetched, because Jesus died on the cross. Yet, the Letter to the Hebrews makes no mistake: God has indeed saved Jesus from death by giving him complete victory over it, but the path to that [victory] is through death itself! The supplication that God has answered referred to Jesus' prayer in Gethsemane. Assailed by looming anguish, Jesus prays to the Father to deliver him of this bitter cup of the Passion, but his prayer is pervaded by trust in the Father, and he entrusts himself entirely to his will: "Not as I will," Jesus says, "but as thou wilt" (Mt 26:39). The object of prayer is of secondary importance; what matters above all is his relationship with the Father. This is what prayer does: it transforms the desire and models it according to the will of God, whatever that may be, because the one who prays aspires first of all to union with God, who is merciful Love.

The parable ends with a question: "When the Son of man comes, will he find faith on earth?" (Lk 18:8). And with this question we are all warned: We must not cease to pray, even if left unanswered. It is prayer that conserves the faith, without it, faith falters! Let us ask the Lord for a faith that is incessant prayer, persevering, like that of the widow in the parable, a faith that nourishes our desire for his coming.

And in prayer let us experience that compassion of God, who like a Father comes to encounter his children, full of merciful love.

## A HUMBLE PRAYER OBTAINS MERCY

Jesus[2] wants to show us the right attitude for prayer and for invoking the mercy of the Father; how one must pray; the right attitude for prayer. It is the parable of the Pharisee and the tax collector (cf. Lk 18:9–14). Both men went up into the Temple to pray, but they do so in very different ways, obtaining opposite results.

The Pharisee stood and prayed using many words. His is yes, a prayer of thanksgiving to God, but it is really just a display of his own merits, with a sense of superiority over "other men," whom he describes as "extortioners, unjust, adulterers, or even," for example, referring to the other one there, "like this tax collector" (v. 11). But this is the real problem: that Pharisee prays to God, but in truth he is just self-lauditory. He is praying to himself! Instead of having the Lord before his eyes, he has a mirror. Although he is standing in the Temple, he doesn't feel the need to prostrate himself before the majesty of God; he remains standing, he feels secure, as if he were the master of the Temple! He lists all the good works he has done: He is beyond reproach, observing the Law beyond measure, he fasts "twice a week" and pays "tithes" on all he possesses. In short, rather than prayer, he is satisfied with his observance of the precepts. Yet, his attitude and his words are far from the way of God's words and actions, the God who loves all men and does not despise sinners. On the contrary, this Pharisee despises sinners, even by indicating the other one there. In short, the Pharisee, who holds himself to be just, neglects the most important commandment: love of God and of neighbor.

It is not enough, therefore, to ask *how much* we pray, we have to ask ourselves *how* we pray, or better, in *what state our heart is*: it is important to examine it so as to evaluate our thoughts, our feelings, and root out arrogance and hypocrisy. But I ask myself: Can one pray with arrogance? No. Can one pray with hypocrisy? No. We must only pray by placing ourselves before God just as we are. Not like the Pharisee who prays with arrogance and hypocrisy. We are all taken up by the frenetic pace of daily life, often at the mercy of feelings, dazed and confused. It is necessary to learn how to rediscover the path to our heart, to recover the value of intimacy and silence, because the God who encounters us and speaks to us is there. Only by beginning there can we in our turn encounter others and speak with them. The Pharisee walked toward the Temple, sure of himself, but he was unaware of the fact that his heart had lost the way.

Instead, the tax collector — the other man — presents himself in the Temple with a humble and repentant spirit: "standing far off, would not even lift up his eyes to heaven, but beat his breast" (v. 13). His prayer was very brief, not long, like that of the Pharisee: "God, be merciful to me a sinner." Nothing more. A beautiful prayer! Indeed, tax collectors — then called "publicans" — were considered impure, subject to foreign rulers; they were disliked by the people and socially associated with "sinners." The parable teaches us that a man is just or sinful not because of his social class but because of his way of relating to God and how he relates to his brothers and sisters. Gestures of repentance and the few and brief words of the tax collector bear witness to his awareness of his own miserable condition. His prayer is essential. He acts out of humility, certain only that he is a sinner in need of mercy. If the Pharisee asked for nothing because he already had everything, the tax collector can only beg for the mercy of God. And this is beautiful: to beg for the mercy of God! Presenting himself with "empty hands," with a bare heart, and acknowledging himself to be a sinner, the tax collector shows us all the condition that is necessary in order to receive the Lord's forgiveness. In the end, he is the one, so despised, who becomes an icon of the true believer.

Jesus concludes the parable with the judgment: "I tell you, this man went down to his house justified rather than the other; for every one who exalts himself will be humbled, but he who humbles himself will be exalted" (v. 14). Of these two, who is the corrupt one? The Pharisee. The Pharisee is the very icon of a corrupt person who pretends to pray but only manages to strut in front of a mirror. He is corrupt and he is pretending to pray. Thus, in life, whoever believes himself to be just and criticizes others and despises them is corrupt and a hypocrite. Pride compromises every good deed, empties prayer, creates distance from God and from others.

If God prefers humility it is not to dishearten us: rather, humility is the necessary condition to be raised by him, so as to experience the mercy that comes to fill our emptiness. If the prayer of the proud does not reach God's heart, the humility of the poor opens it wide. God has a weakness for the humble ones. Before a humble heart, God opens his heart entirely. It is this humility that the Virgin Mary expresses in the Canticle of the *Magnificat*: "He has regarded the low estate of his handmaiden ... his mercy is on those who fear him from generation to generation" (Lk 1:48–50). Let her help us, our Mother, to pray with a humble heart. And we, let us repeat that beautiful prayer three times: "Oh God, be merciful to me, a sinner."

## IT MAKES US SONS AND DAUGHTERS OF THE FATHER

*Our Father.*[3] This is not one of many Christian prayers, but *the prayer of the children of God*: it is the great prayer that Jesus taught us. Indeed, consigned to us on the day of our baptism, the Our Father makes resonate within us those same sentiments that Christ Jesus bore within. When we pray the Our Father, we pray as Jesus prayed. It is the prayer that Jesus prayed, and he taught it to us, when the disciples said to him, "Master, teach us to pray as you pray." And this is how Jesus prayed. It is so beautiful to pray like Jesus! Formed by his divine teaching, we dare to turn to God calling him "Father," because we are reborn as his children through water and the Holy Spirit (cf. Eph 1:5). No one, truly, could call him *Abba* — "Father" — in a familiar way without having been created by God, without the inspiration of the Holy Spirit, as Saint Paul teaches (cf. Rom 8:15). We must consider: No one can call him "Father" without the inspiration of the Spirit. How often there are people who say the Our Father but do not know what they are saying. Because, yes, he is the Father, but when you say "Father," do you feel that he is Father, your Father, the Father of mankind, the Father of Jesus Christ? Do you have a relationship with this Father? When we pray the

Our Father, we connect with the Father who loves us, but it is the Spirit who gives us this connection, this feeling of being God's children.

What better prayer than the one taught by Jesus could prepare us for sacramental Communion with him? Apart from the Mass, the Our Father is prayed in the morning and at night, in praises and in vespers; in this way, the filial attitude toward God and that of fraternity with our neighbor help give Christian form to our days.

In the Lord's Prayer — in the Our Father — we ask for our daily bread, in which we see a particular reference to the Eucharistic bread, which we need in order to live as children of God. We also implore forgiveness of our trespasses. And in order to be worthy to receive God's forgiveness we commit to forgiving those who have offended us. And this is not easy. Forgiving the people who have offended us is not easy; it is a grace that we must ask for: "Lord, teach me to forgive as you have forgiven me." It is a grace. Through our own efforts we are unable: to forgive is a grace of the Holy Spirit. Thus, as we open our heart to God, the Our Father also prepares us for fraternal love. Last, we again ask God to deliver us from evil which separates us from him and divides us from our brothers and sisters. Let us clearly understand that these requests are quite appropriate to prepare ourselves for holy Communion.[4]

Indeed, what we ask in the Our Father is extended by the prayer of the priest who, in the name of all, implores: "Deliver us Lord from every evil, and grant us peace in our day." He then receives a sort of seal in the Rite of Peace: what he first asks of Christ is that the gift of his peace (cf. Jn 14:27) —

thus different from worldly peace — may help the Church to grow in unity and in peace, according to his will; then, with the concrete gesture exchanged among us, we express "ecclesial communion and mutual charity before communicating in the Sacrament."[5] In the Roman rite the exchange of the sign of peace, placed from antiquity before Communion, is ordered to Eucharistic Communion. According to Saint Paul's admonition, it is impossible to communicate with the one bread that renders us one Body in Christ without recognizing that we are reconciled by fraternal love (cf. 1 Cor 10:16–17; 11:29). Christ's peace cannot take root in a heart incapable of experiencing fraternity and of restoring it after it has been wounded. Peace is granted by the Lord: He grants us the grace to forgive those who have offended us.

The gesture of peace is followed by the *Fraction of Bread*.[6] Performed by Jesus during the Last Supper, the breaking of the bread is the revelatory gesture that allowed the disciples to recognize him after his resurrection. We remember the disciples of Emmaus who, in speaking of their encounter with the Risen One, recount "how he was known to them in the breaking of the bread" (cf. Lk 24:30–31, 35).

The breaking of the Eucharistic bread is accompanied by the invocation of the Lamb of God, the figure which John the Baptist indicated in Jesus "who takes away the sin of the world" (Jn 1:29). The biblical image of the lamb speaks of redemption (cf. Ex 12:1–14; Is 53:7; 1 Pt 1:19; Rv 7:14). In the Eucharistic bread, broken for the life of the world, the prayerful assembly recognizes the true Lamb of God — namely, Christ the Redeemer, and implores him, "Have mercy on us ... grant us peace."

"Have mercy on us" and "grant us peace" are invocations that, from the Our Father prayer to the Fraction of Bread, help us to prepare our soul to participate in the Eucharistic banquet, the source of communion with God and with our brothers and sisters.

Let us not forget the great prayer: the one that Jesus taught us, and which is the prayer with which he prayed to the Father. This prayer prepares us for Communion.

# STANDING UP FOR ONE ANOTHER, WITHOUT FAIL

## MARY PRAYS AND TEACHES US HOW TO PRAY

Mary,[1] at the very moment she perceives that there is no wine, approaches Jesus with confidence: this means that *Mary prays*. She goes to Jesus, she prays. She does not go to the steward; she immediately tells her Son of the newlyweds' problem. The response she receives seems disheartening: "What does it have to do with you and me? My hour has not yet come" (Jn 2:4). But she nonetheless places the problem in God's hands. Her deep concern to meet the needs of others hastens Jesus' hour. And Mary was a part of that hour, from the cradle to the cross. She was able "to turn a stable into a home for Jesus, with poor swaddling clothes and an abundance of love" (*Evangelii Gaudium*, 286). She accepted us as her sons and daughters when the sword pierced her heart. She teaches us to put our families in God's hands; she teaches us to pray, to kindle the hope which shows us that our concerns are also God's concerns.

Praying always lifts us out of our worries and concerns. It makes us rise above everything that hurts, upsets, or disappoints us, and helps to put ourselves in the place of others, in their shoes. The family is a school where prayer also reminds us that we are not isolated individuals; we are one, and we have a neighbor close at hand: he or she is living under the same roof, is a part of our life, and is in need. ...

In the family, and we are all witnesses of this, miracles are performed with what little we have, with what we are, with what is at hand ... and many times, it is not ideal, it is not what we dreamt of, nor what "should have been." There is one detail that makes us think: the new wine, that good wine mentioned by the steward at the wedding feast of Cana, came from the water jars, the jars used for ablutions, we might even say from the place where everyone had left their sins ... it came from the "worst" because "where sin increased, grace abounded all the more" (Rom 5:20). In our own families and in the greater family to which we all belong, nothing is thrown away, nothing is useless. Shortly before the opening of the Jubilee Year of Mercy, the Church will celebrate the ordinary synod devoted to the family, deepen her spiritual discernment, and consider concrete solutions and help to the many difficult and significant challenges facing families today. I ask you to pray fervently for this intention, so that Christ can take even what might seem to us impure, like the water in the jars scandalizing or threatening us, and turn it — by making it part of his "hour" — into a miracle. The family today needs this miracle.

All this began because "they had no wine." It could all be done because a woman — the Virgin Mary — was attentive, left her concerns in God's hands, and acted sensibly and courageously. But there is a further detail, the best was to come: Everyone went on to enjoy the finest of wines. And this is the good news: The finest wines are yet to be tasted; for families, the richest, deepest and most beautiful things are yet to come. The time is coming when we will taste love daily, when our children will come to appreciate the home we share, and our elderly will be present each day in the joys of life. The finest of wines is expressed by hope, this wine will come for every person who stakes everything on love. And the best wine is yet to come, in spite of all the variables and statistics which say otherwise. The best wine will come to those who today feel hopelessly lost. Say it to yourselves until you are convinced of it. Say it to yourselves, in your hearts: The best wine is yet to come. Whisper it to the hopeless and the loveless. Have patience, hope, and follow Mary's example; pray, open your heart, because the best wine is yet to come. God always seeks out the peripheries, those who have run out of wine, those who drink only of discouragement. Jesus feels their weakness, in order to pour out the best wines for those who, for whatever reason, feel that all their jars have been broken.

## ONE BODY, ONE SPIRIT, ONE HOPE

Dear[2] brothers and sisters, never forget the call, your first encounter with Jesus, the joy with which you first received the Good News, perhaps from your parents or grandparents, perhaps from your catechists or teachers.

Above all, never stop praying: praying for one another, supporting one another in prayer, and all will see that Jesus, through you and despite your weakness, will accomplish marvelous things in the sight of all his people.

## AGAINST THE EVIL ONE AND FOR THE PASTORS OF THE CHURCH

Among[3] his people, a man aware of being chosen by God, a man of prayer: this is the strength of a bishop ... it is important to remember this, especially at a time when it seems the Great Accuser has been let loose and is on the hunt for bishops. It is true: we bishops are sinners too. [The Great Accuser] seeks to unveil our sins so that they may be seen and scandalize all the people. The Great Accusor who, as he himself says to God in the first chapter of the Book of Job, "roaming the earth and patrolling it." A bishop's greatest strength against the Great Accuser is prayer: the prayer of Jesus and the prayer of the bishop; the humility to know that he has been chosen to remain close to the people of God, refusing to pursue an aristocratic lifestyle unworthy of his consecration. Let us pray today for our bishops: for me, for all of you here, and for bishops throughout the world.

## IN TIMES OF DIFFICULTY

I[4] lived through a time of deep and dark desolation. I thought I had already reached the end. I was acting as confessor, but in a spirit of defeat. Why? Because, even though

I didn't know it at the time (it's only clear to me now), I believed that I was fully living my vocation by doing these kinds of things. But no! There was something else in store for me. I continued to pray, and this was a great help to me. I was really praying a lot, but I still felt like a piece of dry, dead wood. But it is true that prayer was a great help to me: prayer in front of the tabernacle. Then a phone call came from the nuncio, opening the door to a new phase in my life. Yet during the last part of that period — a period of years, though I can't remember exactly how long — perhaps from 1983 to 1992 — prayer was peaceful, very peaceful. So I asked myself, "What could possibly happen now?", because I was feeling different and extremely peaceful. I was acting as confessor and spiritual director: that was my job. But I was carrying out these tasks under a cloud of darkness and suffering; even perhaps with a spirit of infidelity, since I couldn't bring myself to search the right path. I was seeking consolation for the (lost) world of "omnipotence." I was seeking a worldly type of consolation. Nevertheless, in the final part of that period, the Lord was preparing me to receive a telephone call from the nuncio that would put me on an entirely different path. That's the way it was: dark, not easy, but lots of prayer — much prayer — and consolation. That is how I would answer the question about how I lived during that period. In the most recent phase —that is, from 2013 —I really didn't recognize what was happening there. I thought I would just act as I had been: like a bishop. [I said to myself:] "You take care of it! It was you who put me here!"

## PRAYER TO THE FATHER IN A TIME OF TRIAL

Let[5] us pause on some of the words with which Jesus prayed to the Father during his passion.

The first invocation occurs after the Last Supper when the Lord "lifted up his eyes to heaven and said, 'Father, the hour has come; glorify thy Son'" — and then — "glorify thou me in thy own presence with the glory which I had with thee before the world was made" (Jn 17:1–5). Jesus asks for *glory*, a request which seems a paradox as his passion is imminent. What glory is he referring to? In the Bible, glory refers to God's self-revelation. It is the distinctive sign of his saving presence among mankind. Now, Jesus is the One who definitively manifests God's presence and salvation. And he does this at Easter: lifted up on the cross, he is *glorified* (cf. Jn 12:23–33). There, God finally reveals his glory: He removes the last veil and astonishes us as never before. Indeed, we discover that the Glory of God is *entirely love*: pure, unbridled, and inconceivable love, beyond every limit and measure.

Brothers and sisters, let us make Jesus' prayer our own. Let us ask the Father to remove the veil from our eyes, so that in looking at the crucifix over these days we may understand that God is love. How often do we imagine him as master and not as Father; how often do we think of him as an austere judge rather than a merciful Savior! But at Easter, God voids the distances, revealing himself in the humility of a love that seeks our love. Thus we give him glory when we live whatever we do with love, when we do everything from our heart, as if for him (cf. Col 3:17).

True glory is the glory of love because it is the only kind

that gives life to the world. This glory is certainly the opposite of worldly glory, which comes from being admired, praised, acclaimed: when the *I* is at the center of attention. The glory of God, on the other hand, is paradoxical: no applause, no *audience*. At the center is not the I, but rather the other. Indeed, at Easter we see that the Father glorifies the Son as the Son glorifies the Father. No one glorifies himself or herself. We can ask ourselves today: "Which glory do I live for? Mine or God's? Do I wish only to receive from others or also to give to others?"

After the Last Supper, Jesus enters the Garden of Gethsemane and here, too, he *prays to the Father*. While the disciples are unable to stay awake and Judas is approaching with the soldiers, Jesus begins to feel distressed and troubled. He feels all the anguish at what awaits him: betrayal, contempt, suffering, failure. He is sorrowful, and there in the abyss, in that desolation, he addresses the Father with the most tender and gentle word: "*Abba*" — that is, Father (cf. Mk 14:33–36). Jesus teaches us to embrace the Father in our trials, because in praying to him, there is the strength to go forward in suffering. In times of struggle, prayer is relief, entrustment, comfort. Abandoned by all, in inner desolation, Jesus is not alone. He is with the Father. On the other hand, we, in our own Gethsemanes, often choose to remain alone rather than say "Father" and entrust ourselves to him, as Jesus did, entrusting ourselves to his will which is our true good. But when we remain closed within ourselves during trials, we dig a tunnel inside ourselves, a painful, introverted path that has only one direction: ever deeper into ourselves. Solitude does not offer a way out, prayer does, because it is relationship, it is entrustment. Jesus entrusts everything and all of himself to the Father, bringing to him all that he feels, leaning on him in the struggle. When we enter our own Gethsemanes — we each have our own Gethsemanes or have had them or will have them — let us remember this: When we enter, when we will enter our Gethsemane, let us remember to pray in this way: "Father."

Last, Jesus addresses to the Father a third prayer *for us*: "Father, forgive them; for they know not what they do" (Lk 23:34). Jesus prays for those who were cruel to him, for his killers. The Gospel points out that this prayer occurs at the moment of the crucifixion. It was probably the moment of sharpest pain, when nails were being driven into his wrists and feet. Here, at the peak of suffering, comes the pinnacle of love: *forgiveness*, which is the gift to the nth power that breaks the cycle of evil.

As we pray the Lord's Prayer in these days, we can ask for one of these graces: to live our days for the glory of God — that is, to live with love; to know how to entrust ourselves to the Father in times of trial and to utter "dad" to the Father and, in the encounter with the Father, to find forgiveness and the courage to forgive. Both things go together, the Father forgives us, but he gives us the courage to be able to forgive.

## FOR THE SICK

The[6] Church invites constant prayer for her own loved ones stricken with suffering. There must never be a lack of prayer for the sick. But rather, we must pray more, both personally and as a community. Let us consider the Gospel episode of the Canaanite woman (cf. Mt 15:21-28). She is a pagan woman. She is not of the People of Israel, but a pagan who implores Jesus to heal her daughter. To test her faith, Jesus at first responds harshly: "I cannot, I must think first of the sheep of Israel." The woman does not give up — when a mother asks for help for her infant, she never gives up; we all know that mothers fight for their children — and she replies: "Even dogs are given something when their masters have eaten," as if to say: "At least treat me like a dog!" Thus Jesus says to her: "Woman, great is your faith! Be it done for you as you desire" (v. 28).

In the face of illness, even in families, difficulties arise due to human weakness. But in general, times of illness enable family bonds to grow stronger. I think about how important it is to teach children, starting from childhood, about solidarity in times of illness. An education which protects against sensitivity for human illness withers the heart. ...

The weakness and suffering of our dearest and most cherished loved ones can be, for our children and grandchildren, a school of life — it's important to teach the children, the grandchildren to understand this closeness in illness at home — and they become so when times of illness are accompanied by prayer and the affectionate and thoughtful closeness of relatives. The Christian community really knows that the family, in the trial of illness, should not be left on its own. We must say "thank you" to the Lord for those beautiful experiences of ecclesial fraternity that help families get through the difficult moments of pain and suffering. This Christian closeness, from family to family, is a real treasure for the parish; a treasure of wisdom, which helps families in the difficult moments to understand the kingdom of God better than many discourses! They are God's caresses.

## LOSING A LOVED ONE

One[7] way of maintaining fellowship with our loved ones is to pray for them. The Bible tells us that "to pray for the dead" is "holy and pious" (2 Mc 12:44-45). "Our prayer for them is capable not only of helping them, but also of making their intercession for us effective" (*Catechism of the Catholic Church*, 958). The Book of Revelation portrays the martyrs interceding for those who suffer injustice on earth (cf. 6:9-11), in solidarity with this world and its history. Some saints, before dying, consoled their loved ones by promising them that they would be near to help them. Saint Thérèse of Lisieux wished to continue doing good from heaven. Saint Dominic stated that "he would be more helpful after death ... more powerful in obtaining graces."[8] These are truly "bonds of love," because "the union of the wayfarers with the brethren who sleep in the Lord is in no way interrupted ... [but] reinforced by an exchange of spiritual goods" (*Lumen Gentium*, 49).

## IN THE FAMILY

After[9] reflecting on how the family lives the time of celebration and that of work, let us now consider *the time of prayer*. The most frequent complaint of Christians is actually with regard to time: "I should pray more ... I would like to but often I have no time." We hear it all the time. The regret is sincere, certainly, because the human heart always desires prayer, even without realizing it; and if it doesn't find it, it is not at peace. But in order to find it, we need to cultivate in our hearts an "ardent" love for God, an affectionate love.

Let us ask a very simple question. It's good to believe in God with all our heart, it's good to hope that he will help us in difficulty, it's good to feel obliged to give him thanks. All this is just, but *do we love the Lord, even a little*? Does the thought of God move us, amaze us, soften us?

Let us think of the wording of that great commandment, which is the basis of all others: "You shall love the Lord your God with all your heart, and with all your soul, and with all your might" (Dt 6:5; cf. Mt 22:37). The formula uses the intense language of love, addressing it to God. See, the spirit of prayer dwells here above all. And if it dwells here, *it dwells all the time*, and never leaves. Are we able to think of God as the caress that keeps us alive, before which there is nothing? A caress from which nothing, not even death, can separate us? Or do we think of him only as the great Being, the Almighty who made all things, the Judge who monitors every action? All true, of course; but only when God is the affection above all our affections does the meaning of these words find their fullness. Then we feel happy, even if a little confused, because he thinks of us, and above all he loves us! Isn't that impressive? Isn't it impressive that God caresses us with the love of a father? It is so beautiful! He could have simply revealed himself as the Supreme Being, given his commandments, and waited for the results. Instead, God did and does infinitely more than this. He accompanies us on life's journey, he protects us, he loves us.

If love for God does not light the fire, the spirit of prayer will not warm time. We may also multiply our words, as the pagans do, says Jesus; or even perform our rituals, as the Pharisees do (cf. Mt 6:5, 7). A heart which is home to affection for God makes a prayer of an unspoken thought, or an invocation before a holy image, or a kiss blown to the Church. It's beautiful when mothers teach their little children to blow kisses to Jesus or to Our Lady. What tenderness there is in this! In that moment the child's heart is transformed into a place of prayer. And it is a gift of the Holy Spirit. Let us never forget to ask for this gift for each one of us! Because the Spirit of God has that special way of saying in our heart "Abba" — "Father." It teaches us to say "Father" just as Jesus said it, a way that we can never find on our own (cf. Gal 4:6). *It is in the family that one learns to ask for and appreciate this gift of the Spirit.* If one learns to say it with the same spontaneity with which one learns "father" and "mother," one has learnt it forever. When this happens, the time of the whole of family life is enveloped in the womb of God's love and seeks spontaneously the time of prayer.

We know well that family time is a complicated and crowded time, busy and preoccupied. There is always little, there is never enough, there are so many things to do. One who has a family soon learns to solve an equation that not even the great mathematicians know how to solve: within twenty-four hours they make twice that many! There are mothers and fathers who could win the Nobel Prize for this. Out of twenty-four hours they make forty-eight: I don't know how they do it, but they get on and do it! There is so much work in a family!

The spirit of prayer gives time back to God, it steps away from the obsession of a life that is always lacking time, it rediscovers the peace of necessary things, and it discovers the joy of unexpected gifts. Two good guides for this are the sisters Martha and Mary, spoken of in the Gospel; they learned from God the harmony of family rhythms: the beauty of celebration, the serenity of work, the spirit of prayer (cf. Lk 10:38–42). The visit of Jesus, whom they loved, was their celebration. However, one day Martha learned that the work of hospitality, though important, is not everything, but that listening to the Lord, as Mary did, was the really essential thing, the "best kind" of time. Prayer flows from listening to Jesus, from reading the Gospel. Do not forget to read a passage of the Gospel every day. Prayer flows from closeness with the word of God. Is there this closeness in our family? Do we have the Gospel at home? Do we open it sometimes to read it together? Do we meditate on it while reciting the Rosary? The Gospel read and meditated on as a family is like good bread that nourishes everyone's heart. In the morning and in the evening, and when we sit at the table, we learn to say together a prayer with great simplicity: It is Jesus who comes among us, as he was with the family of Martha, Mary, and Lazarus. There is something that is very close to my heart, because I have seen it in the city: There are children who have not learned to make the Sign of the Cross! But you, mother, father, teach your child to pray, to make the Sign of the Cross: this is a lovely task for mothers and fathers!

In the prayer of the family, in its intense moments, and in its difficult seasons, we are entrusted to one another so that each one of us in the family may be protected by the love of God.

## CHRIST ENLIGHTENS THE WHOLE FAMILY LIFE

If[10] a family is centered on Christ, he will unify and illumine its entire life. Moments of pain and difficulty will be experienced in union with the Lord's cross, and his closeness will make it possible to surmount them. In the darkest hours of a family's life, union with Jesus in his abandonment can help avoid a breakup. Gradually, "with the grace of the Holy Spirit, [the spouses] grow in holiness through married life, also by sharing in the mystery of Christ's cross, which transforms difficulties and sufferings into an offering of love."[11] Moreover, moments of joy, relaxation, celebration, and even sexuality can be experienced as a sharing in the full life of the Resurrection. Married couples shape with different daily gestures a "God-enlightened space in which to experience the hidden presence of the risen Lord."[12]

Family prayer is a special way of expressing and strengthening this Paschal faith. A few minutes can be found each day to come together before the living God, to tell him our worries, to ask for the needs of our family, to pray for someone experiencing difficulty, to ask for help in showing love, to give thanks for life and for its blessings, and to ask Our Lady to protect us beneath her maternal mantle. With a few simple words, this moment of prayer can do immense good for our families. The various expressions of popular piety are a treasure of spirituality for many families. The family's communal journey of prayer culminates by sharing together in the Eucharist, especially in the context of Sunday rest. Jesus knocks on the door of families, to share with them the Eucharistic supper (cf. Rv 3:20).

01/18/22

...ET TO PLACE
...H YOUR BOOKS.
...EING A
SENIOR MOMENT;)!

TAKE CARE

Jerry

# IN THE MANY AND VARIED VOCATIONS ...

*There are different kinds of spiritual gifts but the same Spirit; there are different forms of service but the same Lord; there are different workings but the same God who produces all of them in everyone. 1 Corinthians 12:4-6*

## GRANDPARENTS

Dear[1] grandparents, dear elderly, let us follow in the footsteps of these extraordinary elders! Let us too become like poets of prayer. Let us develop a taste for finding our own words. Let us once again grasp those which teach us the

107

word of God. The prayer of grandparents and of the elderly is a great gift for the Church, it is a treasure! A great injection of wisdom for the whole of human society: above all for one which is too busy, too taken, too distracted. Someone should also sing for them too, sing of the signs of God, proclaim the signs of God, pray for them! Let us look to Benedict XVI, who chose to spend the final span of his life in prayer and listening to God! This is beautiful! A great believer of the last century, of the Orthodox tradition, Olivier Clément, said: "A civilization which has no place for prayer is a civilization in which old age has lost all meaning. And this is terrifying. For, above all, we need old people who pray; prayer is the purpose of old age." We need old people who pray because this is the very purpose of old age. The prayer of the elderly is a beautiful thing.

We are able to *thank* the Lord for the benefits received and fill the emptiness of ingratitude that surrounds us. We are able to *intercede* for the expectations of younger generations and give dignity to the memory and sacrifices of past generations. We are able to remind ambitious young people that a life without love is a barren life. We are able say to young people who are afraid that anxiety about the future can be overcome. We are able to teach the young who are overly self-absorbed that there is more joy in giving than in receiving. Grandfathers and grandmothers form the enduring "chorus" of a great spiritual sanctuary, where prayers of supplication and songs of praise sustain the community which toils and struggles in the field of life.

Last, prayer *unceasingly purifies the heart*. Praise and supplication to God prevents the heart from becoming hardened by resentment and selfishness. How awful is the cynicism of an elderly person who has lost the meaning of his testimony, who scorns the young and does not communicate the wisdom of life! How beautiful, however, is the encouragement an elderly person manages to pass on to a young person who is seeking the meaning of faith and of life! It is truly the mission of grandparents, the vocation of the elderly. The words of grandparents have special value for the young. And the young know it. I still carry with me, always, in my breviary, the words my grandmother consigned to me in writing on the day of my priestly ordination. I read them often, and they do me good.

## HUSBANDS AND WIVES

It[2] is also helpful to encourage each of the spouses to find time for prayer alone with God, since each has his or her secret crosses to bear. Why shouldn't we tell God our troubles and ask him to grant us the healing and help we need to remain faithful?

## PARENTS

The[3] home must continue to be the place where we learn to appreciate the meaning and beauty of the Faith, to pray and to serve our neighbor. This begins with baptism, in which, as Saint Augustine said, mothers who bring their children "cooperate in the sacred birthing."[4] Thus begins the journey of growth in that new life. Faith is God's gift, received in baptism, and not our own work, yet parents are the means that God uses for it to grow and develop. Hence "it is beautiful when mothers teach their little children to blow a kiss to Jesus or to Our Lady. How much love there is in that! At that moment the child's heart becomes a place of prayer."[5] Handing on the faith presumes that parents themselves genuinely trust God, seek him and sense their need for him, for only in this way does "one generation laud your works to another, and declare your mighty acts" (Ps 144:4) and "fathers make known to children your faithfulness" (Is 38:19). This means that we need to ask God to act in their hearts, in places where we ourselves cannot reach.

## FOR ONE'S OWN CHILDREN

It[6] is essential that children actually see that, for their parents, prayer is something truly important. Hence moments of family prayer and acts of devotion can be more powerful for evangelization than any catechism class or sermon. Here I would like to express my particular gratitude to all those mothers who continue to pray, like Saint Monica, for their children who have strayed from Christ.

## YOUNG PEOPLE

"Lord[7] Jesus, give me a heart that is free, that I may not be a slave to all the snares in the world. That I may not be a slave to comfort and deception. That I may not be a slave to the good life. That I may not be a slave to vice. That I may not be a slave to a false freedom, which means doing what I want at every moment." Thank you, Orlando, for making us realize that we need to ask God for a heart that is free. Ask him for this everyday! ...

"Lord Jesus, I thank you for being here, I thank you because you gave me brothers and a sister like Manuel, Orlando, and Liz. I thank you because you have given us many brothers and sisters like them. They found you, Jesus. They know you, Jesus. They know that you, their God, are their strength. Jesus, I pray for all those young boys and girls who do not know that you are their strength and who are afraid to live, afraid to be happy, afraid to have dreams. Jesus, teach them how to dream, to dream big, to dream beautiful things, things which, although they seem ordinary, are things which enlarge the heart. Lord Jesus, give us strength. Give us a free heart. Give us hope. Give us love and teach us how to serve. Amen."

## ENGAGED COUPLES

It[8] should be implemented from this perspective, also with the benefit of the simple but intense witness of Christian spouses. And also by focusing on the essentials: the Bible, by consciously rediscovering it together; prayer, in its liturgical dimension, but also in "domestic prayer" to live out in the home, the sacraments, the sacramental life, confession, where the Lord comes to abide in the engaged couple and prepare them truly to receive one another "with the grace of Christ"; and fraternity with the poor and those in need, who lead us to live soberly and to share.

Engaged couples who commit themselves to this path both grow, and all of this leads to preparing for a beautiful celebration of marriage in a different way, not in a worldly way, but in a Christian way! Let us consider these words of God we have heard, when he speaks to his people as bridegroom to his future bride: "I will betroth you to me for ever; I will betroth you to me in righteousness and in justice, in steadfast love, and in mercy. I will betroth you to me in faithfulness; and you shall know the Lord" (Hos 2:19-20). May every engaged couple think of this and say to one another: "I will take you as my bride, I will take you as my bridegroom." Wait for that moment. It is a moment, it is a path that goes slowly ahead, but it is a path of maturation. The steps of the journey should not be rushed. This is how we mature, step by step.

• • •

The[9] couple can also meditate on the biblical readings and the meaningfulness of the rings they will exchange and the other signs that are part of the rite. Nor would it be good for them to arrive at the wedding without ever having prayed together, one for the other, to seek God's help in remaining faithful and generous, to ask the Lord together what he wants of them, and to consecrate their love before an image of the Virgin Mary. Those who help prepare them for marriage should help them experience these moments of prayer that can prove so beneficial.

## ... AND THE MINISTERS OF THE CHURCH
### Bishops

God[10] goes before us. We are only branches; we are not the vine. So do not silence the voice of the One who has called you or delude yourselves into thinking that the success of the mission entrusted to you depends on your own meager virtues — your own — or the benevolence of the powers that be. Instead, pray fervently, indeed fervently, when you have so little to give, so that you will be granted something to offer to those who are close to your hearts as pastors. In the life of a bishop, prayer is the vital sap that passes through the vine, without which the branches wither and bear no fruit. So, keep wrestling with God, even more so in the night of his absence, until he gives you his blessing (cf. Gn 32:25–27). The wounds of that important daily wrestling in prayer will be for you a source of healing. You will be healed by God, so that you can in turn bring healing to others.

## *Priests*

Today,[11] in the Divine Office, the reading from Saint Gregory the Great spoke to us of a priest who is appointed as a watchman in the midst of the people, in order to see from afar whatever approaches.[12] A priest is like this, such is a priest. I refer to the priest who is alert, because one who sleeps, despite how high he may be, sees nothing. Such is a priest. Like the rest of his brothers, he, too, is at the plane of his weakness, of his little strength. But the Lord calls him so he may be elevated, so he may climb the watchtower of prayer, to the heights of God. He calls him to enter a dialogue with him: a dialogue of love, from father to son, from brother to brother, a dialogue in which one feels the beating heart of God and learns to see farther, deeper. I have always been struck by the figure of Moses, who was in the midst of the people, in the midst of the troubles, the struggle with the pharaoh, the serious problems to resolve. How when he stood on the shores of the sea and saw the Pharaoh's army coming: "What do I do now?" A man whom God called to be watchman. He made him climb to the heights and spoke to him face-to-face. What a character, we might have said. What does the Bible say? That he was the humblest man on the face of the earth. There was no other man as humble as Moses. When we let ourselves be elevated to the height of the watchtower of prayer, to intimacy with the Father so as to serve our brothers, the sign is humility. Perhaps you compare yourselves to this. However, when you are a little "cocksure," a bit self-important, it is because we are halfway or we think we can be self-sufficient.

The Lord awaits us in prayer — please, do not neglect it — in the *contemplation* of his word, in the recitation of the Liturgy of the Hours. It is not a good journey when prayer is neglected or, worse yet, abandoning it with the excuse of an all-consuming ministry, because "unless the Lord builds the house, / those who build it labor in vain" (Ps 127:1). It would be a serious error to think that the charism can be kept alive by concentrating on external structures, on the framework, on methods or form. God frees us from the spirit of functionalism. The vitality of the charism takes root in the "love you had at first" (cf. Rv 2:4).

• • •

A priest[13] is a man who gives, a man who pardons. For a priest, this is what the verb "to celebrate" means. You can celebrate Mass every day and still be a man who creates division, spreads gossip, and seethes in jealously. You can be a "criminal" because you kill your brother with your tongue. These are not my words, but those of James the Apostle. Read his letter. Even religious communities can have Mass every day, receive holy Communion, and still hate their brothers and sisters in their heart. A priest is a man of God twenty-four hours a day, not only when he puts on his vestments. The liturgy is to become your life and not just an external ritual. This is why it is crucial to pray to the One about whom we speak, to nourish ourselves with the Word we preach, to adore the bread we consecrate, and to do it every day. Prayer, Word, and Bread. Pino Puglisi, who called these "the three Ps" (*preghiera, parola, pane*), reminds us that they are essential for every priest, every day. They are essential for each consecrated man and woman every day: Prayer, Word, and Bread.

• • •

The priesthood[14] is a way of living. It is a vocation, an imitation of Jesus Christ. But *your* priesthood is unique in the sense that it is unlike the priesthood of any other. Given the rich variety of ways the priesthood may be exercised, I say, "Find your style!" Don't dwell on external circumstances that seem to be insurmountable obstacles. Find your style, your personal way of being a priest!

This style develops within a specific environment. What I mean is this: even though I say it again and again, there is no *cliché* in asserting that the priestly life is without joy unless we take the time for personal prayer, to speak face-to-face with the Lord, talking to him, sharing everything that is going on in our lives. There is no *cliché* in saying this! We cannot marginalize the specific circumstances in which we exercise our priesthood and the style with which we exercise it when we converse with the Lord. When I speak to him, do I ask him the right questions? Or do I just talk to myself, blocked by the seemingly endless impossibilities that bring me down. "Oh well, there is nothing I can do. Everything is a disaster ... there is no way to be an effective priest in this secularized world ... " We go on and on with such complaints and blame the limits imposed on us from the outside. The right question to ask is, "Can *limits* be part of the plan in the same way that desires and aspirations are?"

This is indeed a good question: how are the limits involved in your priestly vocation, in the style with which you live it out? In short: when we ask this question, we dwell too easily on external circumstances, and we often use them as an alibi. Because if we only look at external circumstances, we will never see a way out. Each of us has to seek his own style, the right way to live one's particular priestly vocation. This is why there is no *cliché* in saying that we cannot live the ministry joyfully if we don't make moments for personal prayer, speaking with the Lord face-to-face, sharing our entire lives with him. We must bring everything to prayer with the Lord. If you do not dialogue with the Lord, you cannot move forward. Talk to him about your limitations! Ask him for help in identifying your limitations! This is precisely why the help of a spiritual director is necessary; a wise man who can help you in your discernment. For young clergy — and for some older clergy — it is also becoming more popular to meet in small groups. This is also extremely helpful. It is the apex of priestly fraternity: meeting together to talk about how things are going. This is an important part of our priestly rhythm. Living in complete solitude is never a good thing. ...

This is what I would like to emphasize most: Be careful not to get caught up in your limitations. "There's simply no way! Just look around! The world is in chaos because of this or that. Just look at the television!" There are always cultural and personal limits, but it is never right to focus on them. The right way is as I've said. Jesus Christ and prayer must always be the center of your priestly existence.

• • •

I[15] have three suggestions for this day of retreat. ...

The first has to do with two practical counsels that Saint Ignatius gives, and I apologize for the "in house" advertising. He tells us that "it is not great knowledge that fills and satisfies the soul, but the ability to feel and savor the things of God interiorly" (*Spiritual Exercises*, 2). Saint Ignatius adds that whenever we encounter and savor something we desire, we should pray in peace, "without being anxious to move forward as long as I am satisfied" (ibid., 76). So, too, in these meditations on mercy we can begin with what we savor most and linger there, for surely one work of mercy will lead us to others. If we start by thanking the Lord for having wondrously created us and for even more wondrously redeemed us, surely this will lead us to a sense of sorrow for our sins. If we start by feeling compassion for the poor and the outcast, surely we will come to realize that we ourselves stand in need of mercy.

My second suggestion for your prayer has to do with the way we speak about mercy. By now you have realized that in Spanish I like to use "mercy" as a verb: We have to show mercy [*misericordiar* in Spanish — *to mercify*: we have to stretch the language a little] in order to receive mercy [*ser misericordiados — to be mercified*]." "But Father, this is not a real word!" — "True, but it is the form I have found useful to grasp this reality: to show mercy, *misericordiar* and receive mercy, *ser misericordiados.*" Mercy joins a human need to the heart of God, and this leads to immediate action. We cannot meditate on mercy without it turning into action. In prayer, it doesn't help to intellectualize things. With the help of grace, our dialogue with the Lord has to focus straight-away on that sin for which I most need the Lord's mercy, the one of which I am most ashamed, the one for which I most desire to make reparation. From the outset, too, we have to speak of what most moves us, of all those faces that make us want to do something to satisfy their hunger and thirst for God, for justice, for tenderness. Mercy is contemplated in action, but in a kind of action that is all-inclusive. Mercy engages our whole being — our feelings and our spirit — and all other beings as well.

My last suggestion for today's retreat has to do with the fruit of these exercises — namely, the grace that we ask to receive. It is, in a word, the grace to become priests ever more ready to receive mercy (*misericordiados*) and to show mercy (*misericordiosos*). One of the most beautiful things, and which moves me, is a priest's confession: it is something great, beautiful, because this man who comes to confess his own sins is the same who will listen to the heart of other penitents who come to confess their sins. We can concentrate on mercy because it is what is most essential and definitive. By the stairway of mercy (cf. *Laudato Si'*, 77), we can descend to the depths of our human condition — including our frailty and sin — and ascend to the heights of divine perfection: *Be merciful (perfect) as your Father is merciful.* But always for the sake of "reaping" even greater mercy. This fruit should also be seen in a conversion of our institutional mindset: Unless our structures are vibrant and aimed at making us more open to God's mercy and more merciful to others, they can turn into something very bizarre and eventually counterproductive.

## *Deacons*

In[16] today's world it seems that everything is supposed to serve us, and everything is meant for the individual. Prayer is for my sake, the community is for my sake, charity is for my sake. We take that attitude for granted. You, my friends, are the gift of the Holy Spirit who make us see that the real truth is the opposite: I serve in prayer, I serve in community, and in a spirit of solidarity, I serve God and neighbor. May God give you the grace to grow in this charism and to safeguard a spirit of service in the Church.

• • •

Each[17] of us is very dear to God, who loves us, chooses us, and calls us to serve. Yet each of us needs first to be healed inwardly. To be ready to serve, we need a healthy heart: a heart healed by God, one which knows forgiveness and is neither closed nor hardened. We would do well each day to pray trustingly for this, asking to be healed by Jesus, to grow more like him who "no longer calls us servants but friends" (cf. Jn 15:15). Dear deacons, this is a grace you can implore daily in prayer. You can offer the Lord your work, your little inconveniences, your weariness, and your hopes in an authentic prayer that brings your life to the Lord and the Lord to your life. When you serve at the table of the Eucharist, there you will find the presence of Jesus, who gives himself to you so that you can give yourselves to others.

## Religious men and women

Dwelling[18] in and contemplating his divinity by making prayer a fundamental part of our lives and our apostolic service, prayer frees us from the burden of worldliness, and teaches us to live joyfully, to distance ourselves from superficiality, in an exercise of true freedom. In prayer we grow in freedom, in prayer we learn to be free. Prayer draws us out of our self-centeredness, from being reclusive in an empty religious experience; it leads us to place ourselves, with docility, in the hands of God in order to fulfil his will and to realize his plan of salvation. In prayer. And I want to offer you some advice here: ask, contemplate, thank, intercede, but also be familiar with the need *to adore*. It is not very fashionable to adore. Grow accustomed to adoring. To learn to adore in silence. Learn to pray in this way.

## Seminarians and young religious

There[19] are four pillars of formation: study, prayer, pastoral activity, and community life, and the seminary plays a key role in fostering these. A wise bishop once told me: "A bad seminary is better than no seminary at all." This is because community life helps us: it is a propedeutic step toward priestly fraternity. Study, prayer, pastoral activity, and community life are interrelated, because you should pray about the things you study and see in pastoral life on the weekends, and the things that happen in community. Prayer must involve every aspect of our lives since it is related to everything we do and everything that happens to us. This means the four pillars are constantly interacting with one another and never self-standing entities in themselves. There is a unity to these four pillars of formation. When you meet with your spiritual director or your formation adviser or rector, or the superior of the community, you should talk about all four of these pillars and how they are interacting. You should seek with his help to understand how they are related. I don't know if I am being clear ... am I? Yes, there are four, but you have to speak about the relationship between all four of them.

• • •

This[20] is the spirituality [of the diocesan priest]: the relationship with the bishop, the relationship among you, and the contact, the relationship with the People of God with the memory — where I come from — and in service — where I am going. And how does one make this grow? With the spiritual life. You have a spiritual father: Open your heart to the spiritual father. And he will teach you how to pray, prayer; how to love Our Lady: Do not forget this, because she is always close to the vocation of each of you. The meeting with the spiritual father. Who is not an inspector of conscience; he is one who, on behalf of the bishop, helps you to grow.

• • •

The[21] seminary is the school of this fidelity, which is learned first and foremost in prayer, particularly in liturgical prayer. In this time, friendship with Jesus is cultivated, centered on the Eucharist and nourished by contemplation and by the study of Sacred Scripture. The ministry cannot be exercised well if we do not live in union with Christ. Without him we can do nothing (cf. Jn 15:5).

• • •

Always[22] listen and ask for the grace to discern your feelings so as to discover God's will; and correct yourself when things are going badly or aren't working. And never do it alone, but always in company with others. And fraternity — I saw one of the questions dealt with this — there needs to be fraternity with your friends and with the priests around you. But there is another fraternal relationship you must work hard to maintain: fraternity with a priest or monk or layperson whom God has given to you as your spiritual companion in spiritual direction. Because spiritual direction is a lay charism too, no? It's not necessarily something just for priests, because lay people can be spiritual directors, too. It is something priestly, but only insofar as it is "lay." It takes courage to have someone to accompany you on the spiritual journey; to be aware of your interior life, your fidelity, and your infidelity. "Yes, Father, I am always going to confession." But a confessor is something else. It's someone you go to to tell your sins, to receive pardon, and to leave it all there. It is quite another thing to have someone *accompany* you: these are two different things. It's all the better when these two roles are performed by two different individuals. Your confessor has one particular role and your spiritual director another. The latter does not necessarily have to be a priest. It can be a monk or anyone who is spiritually wise. But your spiritual director has to have the charism to accompany you. But if you remain stubborn and go it alone, or if you seek out a director whom you can just joke around with; and then if you are lacking the capacity to connect with others in community or to accompany others, or if your refuse to listen to others, then you'll always be stuck. The capacity to listen is precisely where real prayer starts. How do you pray? Like a parrot? Or do you pray with your thoughts, following wherever your mind leads and confusing prayer with following your own thoughts? Do you know how to pray in silence so that you can listen?

# THE BREATH OF NEW LIFE*

Baptism is the beginning of *new life*. But what does new life mean?

The "newness" of baptism is not like the newness of changing jobs or moving from one town to another. In these situations, we often say, "I've begun a new life," but we mean something quite different. It's true that life changes when we start a new job or move. In fact, it changes a lot. It might be better or worse, more interesting or more boring, depending on the situation. The neighborhood, the surroundings, our colleagues, and even our friendships may change. We live in a different house and earn a different salary. But this is not really a new life. It is the same life as before, only changed.

* Previously unpublished text by Pope Francis

The *new life* of baptism is even different from the radical change of feelings we have when we fall in love, or are disappointed by love, or when we are sick or encounter an unexpected situation.

Such changes can hit us like an earthquake, both inside and outside. They can change our values and our fundamental attitude toward our feelings, work, health, and service to others. At first, we may have been concerned only with our career, but then we start to volunteer, perhaps even making our own life a gift to others! At first, perhaps we gave no thought to building a family, but then we experience the beauty of conjugal and familial love.

Even such major, extraordinary changes are "only" various kinds of transformation. They modify our existing life and bring it to a more beautiful and dynamic level, or perhaps to a more difficult and boring level. When we tell others about such changes, it is perfectly reasonable to speak of them in terms of "more" and "less." Perhaps they have made our lives more beautiful, joyful, or passionate. This is because, despite the change, we are still making comparisons to things that are largely similar. It's as if we simply measure things on a scale of value. Before, I rated the level of happiness in my life at 5, but now I give it a 7. Perhaps I used to give my health a rating of 9, but now I give it a 4. We can change the number, but we can't change the *substance* of our lives.

But the new life of baptism is not new merely with respect to the past — to our previous life or to how things were before. *New* does not mean "recent"; it doesn't mean there has only been some kind of alteration or change.

### *The life of God is a communion that has been given to us in friendship*

The "new life" about which Paul speaks in his letters reminds us of Jesus' new commandment in John 13:34. It reminds us of the new wine of the kingdom (cf. Mk 14:29), the new song sung by the redeemed before God's throne (cf. Rv 5:9); the new, definitive realities that in theological terms we call "eschatological."

These realities help us understand that it is impossible to compare satisfactorily the new life of baptism to any other reality. Can we possibly compare life to death, or life before and after birth? Christ did not become one of us — he did not undertake his passion, death, and resurrection — to "improve" our lives, to make them prettier, spicier, longer, more intense, or easier. As he tells us, he came "so that we might have life, and have it abundantly" (Jn 10:10).

This is new life; the life that God the Father gives us in baptism. It is "new" because it is a life wholly different from our own. It is *his* life, the very life of God. This is the awesome gift that Jesus has given us and continues to give us! The gift of participating in the love of the Father, Son, and Holy Spirit. The gift of participating in the love that the Triune God gave to all men and to all creation. New life is the life of God given to us!

We Christians have always searched for images and symbols to express this immense gift. We are all very different, yet we are all one thing: We are the Church. The unity of the Church is the unity of love: a love that doesn't constrict, humiliate, or limit us. It is a love that strengthens us. It builds us up and makes us all friends.

Jesus gives us a beautiful expression in the Gospel: "This is eternal life: that they may know you, the one, true God, and him whom you have sent" (Jn 17:3). He himself tells us that true life is encountering God; and that to encounter God is to know God.

We also know from the Bible that "to know a person" doesn't mean simply to know him or her with our head, because it implies loving that person. And this is the life of God that has been given to us: the love that becomes *our* love. The love that makes us grow step by step with the grace of the Holy Spirit (cf. Rom. 5:5). The love that infuses the "Please?", "May I?", and "Pardon me" we utter every day.

Even though words fall short, we can say that new life is *to discover Someone, to belong to Someone,* and through him to *belong to everyone.* To belong means that each and everyone "is for the other."

This reminds me of something the bride says in the Song of Songs: "My beloved is mine and I am his" (2:16). Behold, day after day, the Holy Spirit is bringing Jesus' prayer to the Father to its fulfillment: "I pray not only for them, but also for those who will believe in me through their word, so that they may all be one, as you, Father, are in me and I in you, that they also may be in us, that the world may believe that you sent me" (Jn 17:20–21).

One of the most ancient images used to express this belonging, this "living with" — an image highly favored by Saint Paul — is the "body," of which Christ is the head and we are the members: "Now you are Christ's body, and individually parts of it" (1 Cor 12:27).

## The symbol of the body

Some functions of the human body are essential, such as the beating of the heart and breathing.

I like to think of our personal and communal prayer as Christians as the "breath," or the "heartbeat," of the Church that gives each and everyone the strength to serve, to study, to teach. The strength that enlightens both the learned and the unlearned with knowledge. The strength that gives hope and tenacity to those who fight against injustice.

Prayer is our saying "yes" to the Lord, to his love that comes to us. It is our acceptance of the Holy Spirit who, never growing tired, showers each of us with love and life.

Saint Seraphim of Sarov, a great spiritual master of the Russian Church, said, "to acquire the Holy Spirit is the ultimate goal of our Christian life, the point of all our prayer, vigils, fasting, almsgiving, and all other virtuous actions we do in the name of Christ: they are nothing but a means to this end."[1] We are not always conscious of breathing, but we can never stop breathing.

## Prayer and prayers

Hence our breathing is not always the same: sometimes it is calm, sometimes difficult; sometimes our breathing is fast, and at other times we are breathless. Sometimes — such as when the air is clean and crisp in the mountains or at the seashore — breathing is truly a pleasure. How a breath of fresh air renews us in so many ways!

In any case, the important thing to note is that we don't breathe occasionally, [only] once a week or a couple of hours a day. We are *always* breathing! And this *constancy* of breath makes me think of what Saint Paul said: "Pray constantly!" (1 Thes 5:17).

Saint Paul's admonition has been taken seriously in a variety of ways. In some monastic communities, the members took turns day and night, praying uninterruptedly so that the praise of God might never cease.

Both in the East and West the great teachers of Christian prayer have taught us that continual prayer means to live in the Lord's presence always, conversing with him in our hearts and minds. "To pray unceasingly means to have our minds turned to God in fervent love, always eager for the promise of hope that we have in him in everything we do and everything that happens to us."[2]

One thing is clear: just as we are more aware of our breath at times, sometimes we are more conscious about our dialogue with God. These are what we call *moments of prayer:* liturgical, communal, or personal in the silence of our own room (cf. Mt 6:6). Yet these moments do not exhaust what we mean by "prayer." They are simply privileged moments within a twenty-four-hour day entirely spent with the Lord, because we are always breathing. In the end, as Saint Paul says, paradise is "to always be with the Lord" (cf. 1 Thes 4:17). By Jesus' resurrection and our baptism, we have already entered paradise, because we are sons and daughters of the Father: always in his presence, because he never abandons us. His love is immense and ever faithful!

### It is always an encounter, even if no words are spoken

Hence to pray always and to live continuously in the Lord's

presence does not mean reciting formulas, ejaculatory prayers, or simple invocations over and over again. There are times when we lack words and our prayer becomes "inexpressible groans" (cf. Rom 8:26) inspired by the Holy Spirit, who is our teacher in prayer. When we pray, sometimes we cry. Sometimes we laugh. Sometimes our prayer consists of praise, sometimes supplication. Sometimes we focus on thanksgiving, sometimes we ask for pardon. Sometimes we beg the Lord to shed light on a doubt or uncertainty. Sometimes we ask for perseverance when we encounter problems.

Just like relationships with other human beings, prayer does not always consist in words, but it is always a genuine encounter that brings us truly in the presence of the Lord who is always with us (cf. Mt 28:20) and who always gives us his love, mercy, and hope, even when he reproves us or gnaws at our conscience to spark a conversion of heart. His silence is also priceless, because even in that silence there is a gift, a grace — perhaps a hidden grace — of the Spirit who unites us to him and to others. Love is not only expressed in words, but in silence. Love fills silence. Love needs moments of silence.

### In the rhythm of Jesus' paschal mystery
When prayer is a breath of *new life,* it places us in a relationship with the Father. As Blessed Charles de Foucault said, when prayer is authentic, we are more open to the Holy Spirit who, like a master artist,[3] *restores* within us the resemblance of Jesus, our common Brother.

Obviously, the Holy Spirit does not make us resemble Jesus physically. Rather, as Saint Paul says, it makes "the same sentiments" grow to maturity within us (cf. Phil 2:5). It gives us the mindsight and worldview of Jesus.

For Jesus, life is a gift accepted and given. This is the meaning of the paschal mystery of his passion and death through which, in fidelity to the Father, he brought to fulfillment in the resurrection.

Prayer nourishes within us our vocation to follow Jesus Christ in this paschal journey; to entrust and immerse ourselves completely in his death, which, if we stay close to him, becomes the final step to the resurrection and new life.

To test whether our prayer unites us to the Lord, as Saint Ignatius of Loyola reminds us in the *Spiritual Exercises,* we have to verify whether the Paschal mindset is growing within us. If Jesus' paschal mystery is no longer something that has simply happened to *him*, but becomes *our* way of looking at ourselves and the people around us, at the world in which we live, then, with the help of the Holy Spirit, we can say with the Lord: "No one takes (life) from me: I give it myself. I have the power to give it and the power to take it up again." (Jn 10:18). This is the mind of the Church, of the holy and faithful People of God. This is the logic of the saints, including those who live "next door" (cf. *Gaudete et Exsultate,* 6–9).

*New life* really takes root in us when we begin to live *like* God by giving ourselves. This does not happen as a fruit of our virtue or personal merits (because our virtues are always few and unstable), but from the fact that we accept his love more and more each day. His is an active, powerful love that renews us from the inside, unites us to Christ so that we become more like him every day: in our thoughts, feelings, ideals, and love!

Sooner or later, this journey of intimate union with the Lord will bring us to renounce ourselves: this is the "diluted" love of gestures and the attention we give to others, the renunciation of our prejudices and egoism hidden behind nice thoughts and good intentions. In that last breath of faith, we will make our ultimate resignation to the Father!

## *A gift entrusted to us*

These deaths — however big or little — to selfishness are a "warm-up" to grow in *new life*, which was truly given to us, but was also entrused to our care. Step by step, we begin to gain an experience of the Church. Thanks to the death and resurrection of Jesus, the little deaths and death itself become opportunities to make a gift of ourselves, to live in communion and unity: not because we are good, but because we are members of the Body which is Christ and his Church.

This life is truly *new* because, through the paschal mystery, death is *new* — that is, death becomes something entirely different. Death is no longer *the* end, but rather the decisive moment of fidelity to the Father who cares for us (cf. 1 Pt 5, 7). Even if we don't always recognize it, he is always leading us to his kingdom and to communion, ministering to us often through the hands of those around us. Those hands are not always "golden," for neither are our hands always golden. All of us are both saints and sinners, a little generous and a little selfish.

## *Everything is renewed*

A final image comes to mind. Our life is like an hourglass.

The upper part represents our everyday life. Whenever we perform an act of love or give up our prejudices for the sake of love, a grain of sand passes from the upper part to the lower part, which represents eternal life: union with the Lord and with our brothers and sisters. Little by little, everything we are passes from the upper part to the lower part. The years go on, many things change, our bodies weaken, but our efforts to love authentically do not fade or pass away in vain. They rather *pass over into the Lord*. In fact, if united to Christ, whatever passes through the bottleneck of death — just as through the bottleneck of an hourglass — never disappears. It is never annihilated, but always accepted, renewed, and enlivened by the Lord.

There is an important caveat. The Lord is not like an accountant to whom we entrust our wealth so he may give it back with interest in the next life. A life lived out of love for the Lord is not stored up in isolation. It is rather *given back to us* in each and every holy Mass, our greatest participation in Jesus' paschal mystery. In the Mass we see that the truest part of us — the part that has lived in love and mercy — is "hidden with Christ in God" (Col 3:3), because the *law* of friendship is observed precisely by walking with the Church.

The Eucharist is truly the Church's most august sacrament, a revelation that we are always one in the Lord. This is how Saint Augustine explained it: "If, therefore, you are the body of Christ and its members, the mystery of who you are is placed on the altar of the Lord. So receive your mystery! You respond 'Amen' to who you are. And when you respond, you do it with all your heart. What you say 'Amen' to is precisely 'the Body of Christ.' So be true members of Christ's body so that your 'Amen' may ring true!"[4]

Nothing of us is lost. Nothing in us is indifferent or unimportant. To the contrary. Our entire being — our history, our behavior, our dreams, our feelings, our defects, our gifts — if they enter into the realm of love, will pass along the way of Jesus' paschal mystery; and by doing so, we go beyond death and enter the resurrection that creates communion: *this* is the meaning of *new life!*

Francis

# NOTES

## Preface
[1]*De Instituto christiano*, PG 46, 280 B-D.

## A Few Sentences on Prayer
[1]Daily Meditation in the Chapel of Domus Sanctae Marthae, September 3, 2018.
[2]Tweet, May 24, 2013.
[3]Tweet, July 8, 2013.
[4]Address to Superior Generals, February 11, 2017.
[5]Speech to the Italian Bishops' Conference, May 16, 2016.
[6]Ibid.
[7]*Amoris Laetitia*, 227.
[8]Daily Meditation in the Chapel of Domus Sanctae Marthae, October 11, 2018.
[9]Address to a group of young people from the Diocese of Grenoble-Vienne, September 17, 2018.

## United with Jesus
[1]Address to the Pastors of Rome, March 2, 2017.
[2]General Audience, February 14, 2018.
[3]Morning meditation in the Chapel of Domus Sanctae Marthae, October 10, 2013.
[4]Morning meditation in the Chapel of Domus Sanctae Marthae, October 9, 2014.
[5]Morning meditation in the Chapel of Domus Sanctae Marthae, June 20, 2013.
[6]Address to Priests, Religious, and Seminarians in Havana, September 20, 2015.
[7]Angelus, July 24, 2016.
[8]Interview with Father Spadaro in *La Civiltà Cattolica*, III (2013), 476–477.
[9]General Audience, November 15, 2017.
[10]Homily at Vespers, Asunción, Paraguay, July 11, 2015.
[11]Address to members of the General Chapter of the Claretian Fathers, September 11, 2015.
[12]Address to members of the Padre Pio prayer group, February 6, 2016.
[13]Daily meditation in the Domus Sanctae Marthae, January 12, 2018.
[14]Angelus, October 20, 2013.

## Wherever You Are, Pray to the Father
[1]General Audience, December 5, 2018.
[2]General Audience, December 12, 2018.
[3]General Audience, January 2, 2019.

[4]General Audience, January 9, 2019.
[5]General Audience, January 16, 2019.
[6]General Audience, February 13, 2019.
[7]General Audience, February 20, 2019.
[8]General Audience, February 27, 2019.
[9]General Audience, March 6, 2019.
[10]General Audience, March 20, 2019.
[11]General Audience, March 27, 2019.
[12]General Audience, April 10, 2019.
[13]General Audience, April 24, 2019.
[14]General Audience, May 1, 2019.
[15]General Audience, May 15, 2019.
[16]General Audience, May 22, 2019.

## A Transforming Encounter

[1]General Audience, May 26, 2016.
[2]General Audience, June 1, 2016.
[3]General Audience, March 14, 2018.
[4]Cf. General Instruction of the Roman Missal, 81.
[5]Cf. GIRM, 82.
[6]Cf. GIRM, 83; *Catechism of the Catholic Church*, 1329.

## Standing Up for One Another, Without Fail

[1]Homily, Mass at Samanes Park, Guayaquil, Ecuador, July 6, 2015.
[2]To Attendees of the 4th National Congress for Missionary Groups, Santiago del Estero, Argentina, October 10, 2015.
[3]Daily Mediation, Domus Sanctae Marthae, September 11, 2018.
[4]To the Pastors of Rome, March 16, 2018.
[5]General Audience, April 17, 2019. This catechesis was given within a cycle of General Audiences dedicated to the Lord's Prayer. Even though, in this case, the specific theme was "temptation," the passage seems pertinent to prayer and the spiritual life.
[6]General Audience, June 10, 2015.
[7]*Amoris Laetitia*, 257.
[8]Giordano di Sassonia, *Libellus de Principiis Ordinis Praedicatorum*, 93: *Monumenta Historica Sancti Patris Nostri Dominici*, XVI (Rome, 1935), 69.
[9]General Audience, August 26, 2015.
[10]*Amoris Laetitia*, 317–18.
[11]Synod of Bishops, *Relatio Finalis* (2015), 87.
[12]John Paul II, *Vita Consecrata*, 42.

## In the Many and Varied Vocations ...

[1]General Audience, March 11, 2015.

[2]*Amoris Laetitia*, 227.

[3]*Amoris Laetitia*, 287.

[4]*On Holy Virginity*, 7, 7: PL 40, 400.

[5]Catechesis, August 26, 2015.

[6]*Amoris Laetitia*, 288.

[7]Encounter with Young People, Asunción, Paraguay, July 12, 2015.

[8]General Audience, May 27, 2015.

[9]*Amoris Laetitia*, 216.

[10]Address to the Bishops of Colombia, Bogotá, Colombia, September 7, 2017.

[11]Address to Members of the General Chapter of the Schönstatt Movement, September 3, 2015.

[12]Cf. Homily on Ezekiel, 1, 11, 4.

[13]Address to Clergy, Religious, and Seminarians, Palermo, Italy, September 15, 2018.

[14]Address to the Pastors of Rome, February 15, 2018.

[15]Spiritual Retreat for Priests celebrating their Jubilee, Basilica of Saint John Lateran, June 2, 2016.

[16]Address to Priests and Religious; response to a question regarding the permanent diaconate, Milan, Italy, March 25, 2017.

[17]Homily at the Mass for the Jubilee of Deacons, May 29, 2016.

[18]Address to Priests, Consecrated Men and Women, Seminarians, and Their Families, Medellín, Colombia, September 9, 2017.

[19]Address to Seminarians in Lombardy, October 12, 2018.

[20]Address to Seminarians in the Diocese of Agrigento, November 24, 2018.

[21]Address to Seminarians at the Pontifical Seminary of Sardo, February 17, 2018.

[22]Address to Students at the ecclesiastical Pontifical Colleges of Rome, March 16, 2018.

## The Breath of New Life

[1]Seraphim of Sarov, *Conversation with Motovilov*.

[2]Maximus the Confessor, *On Asceticism*, 25.

[3]"Just as a royal portrait is painted with visible colors, so the hidden portrait of our hidden King is painted with visible oil on those who are sealed with it. Baptism, which is the whole reason they came forth from the womb, paints a new portrait to repair the image of Adam that was corrupted. It gives them a new birth in the three gifts accompanied by the three glorious names of Father, Son, and Holy Spirit." (Ephaim of Syria, *Hymns for Virginity*, 7, 5).

[4]Homilies, 272.

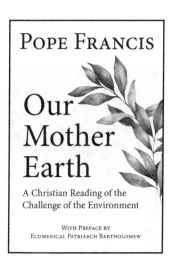

POPE FRANCIS

Our
Mother
Earth

A Christian Reading of the
Challenge of the Environment

WITH PREFACE BY
ECUMENICAL PATRIARCH BARTHOLOMEW

Gathered from the writings and discourses of Pope Francis on the environment, *Our Mother Earth* sets forth a Christian vision of ecology. Responding to our global ecological crisis, Pope Francis says, will require a global approach in which "the whole human family in the search for a sustainable and integral development" unites to protect our common home.

In an exclusive new essay that concludes Our Mother Earth, Pope Francis develops a "theology of ecology" in a profoundly spiritual discourse. This final chapter offers thoughts on how a Christian vision of care for the earth goes well beyond a secular vision of ecology.

**Order today on Amazon
or OSVCatholicBookstore.com**

LAUDATO SI'

ON CARE FOR
OUR COMMON HOME

ENCYCLICAL LETTER
Includes Discussion Questions

POPE FRANCIS

In his second encyclical, *Laudato Si': On Care for Our Common Home*, Pope Francis draws all Christians into a dialogue with every person on the planet about our common home. We as human beings are united by the concern for our planet, and every living thing that dwells on it, especially the poorest and most vulnerable.

Included discussion questions make this book perfect for individual or group study, leading all Catholics and Christians into a deeper understanding of the importance of this teaching.

**Order today on Amazon
or OSVCatholicBookstore.com**

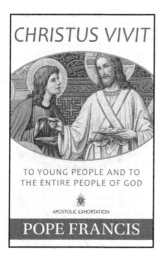

To young Christians of the world, Pope Francis has a message for you: "Christ is alive, and he wants you to be alive!" In his fourth apostolic exhortation, *Christus Vivit*, Pope Francis writes of his fatherly love for young people, the difficult issues they face in the world today, and the truth of the Gospel.

*Christus Vivit* is written for and to young people, but Pope Francis also wrote it for the entire Church, because, as he says, reflecting on our young people inspires us all.

In this apostolic exhortation, *Querida Amazonia* ("The Beloved Amazon"), Pope Francis offers a response to the Synod of Bishops for the Amazon held in Rome in October 2019 and its final document *The Amazon: New Paths for the Church and for an Integral Ecology.*

The pope writes this exhortation to all the faithful calling us to the task of addressing the serious social, environmental, and spiritual issues facing the region. Pope Francis asks: "How can we not struggle together? How can we not pray and work together, side by side, to defend the poor of the Amazon region, to show the sacred countenance of the Lord, and to care for his work of creation?"

**Order today on Amazon
or OSVCatholicBookstore.com**